The
Goodly Fellowship
of the Prophets

Acadia Studies in Bible and Theology

Craig A. Evans and Lee Martin McDonald, General Editors

The last two decades have witnessed dramatic developments in biblical and theological study. Full-time academics can scarcely keep up with fresh discoveries, recently published primary texts, ongoing archaeological work, new exegetical proposals, experiments in methods and hermeneutics, and innovative theological syntheses. For students and nonspecialists, these developments are confusing and daunting. What has been needed is a series of succinct studies that assess these issues and present their findings in a way that students, pastors, laity, and nonspecialists will find accessible and rewarding. Acadia Studies in Bible and Theology, sponsored by Acadia Divinity College in Wolfville, Nova Scotia, and in conjunction with the college's Hayward Lectureship, constitutes such a series.

The Hayward Lectureship has brought to Acadia many distinguished scholars of Bible and theology, such as Sir Robin Barbour, John Bright, Leander Keck, Helmut Koester, Richard Longenecker, Martin Marty, Jaroslav Pelikan, Ian Rennie, James Sanders, and Eduard Schweizer. The Acadia Studies in Bible and Theology series reflects this rich heritage.

These studies are designed to guide readers through the ever more complicated maze of critical, interpretative, and theological discussion taking place today. But these studies are not introductory in nature; nor are they mere surveys. Authored by leading authorities in the field, the Acadia Studies in Bible and Theology series offers critical assessments of the major issues that the church faces in the twenty-first century. Readers will gain the requisite orientation and fresh understanding of the important issues that will enable them to take part meaningfully in discussion and debate.

The
Goodly Fellowship
of the Prophets

The Achievement
of Association in Canon Formation

CHRISTOPHER R. SEITZ

Baker Academic
a division of Baker Publishing Group
Grand Rapids, Michigan

Published by Baker Academic
a division of Baker Publishing Group
P.O. Box 6287, Grand Rapids, MI 49516-6287
www.bakeracademic.com

Printed in the United States of America

Library of Congress Cataloging-in-Publication Data
Seitz, Christopher R.
    The goodly fellowship of the prophets : the achievement of association in canon formation / Christopher R. Seitz.
        p.   cm. — (Acadia studies in Bible and theology)
    Lectures given at Acadia Divinity College, Nova Scotia, fall of 2007 and also an earlier version of these lectures was prepared for Golden Gate Baptist Seminary the same year.
    Includes bibliographical references and index.
    ISBN 978-0-8010-3883-9 (pbk.)
    1. Bible. O.T.—Canon. 2. Bible. O.T. Prophets—Criticism, Textual. 3. Bible—Canonical criticism. 4. Bible. N.T.—Relation to the Old Testament. 5. Bible. O.T.—Relation to the New Testament. I. Title.
BS1135.S45 2009
221.1′2—dc22   2009011840

In memoriam
Brevard Springs Childs
(1923–2007)

Contents

I have adapted the lectures as given only minimally. They constitute the contents of the three main chapters. To produce a book of sufficient length for the present series, however, I have also drawn up a general introduction to the topic. Following the introduction, chapter 1 begins as the first lecture of the series proper and concludes with some explanatory notes as to why I am dealing with the topic I have chosen. Beyond that, there should be very minimal overlap, and I hope the book as a whole addresses the general theme of canon formation in the Old Testament in a straightforward and useful way.

I am also presently completing a book on the relationship between the Testaments and the exegetical and hermeneutical significance of the rule of faith in the early church, which is scheduled to appear in Baker Academic's Studies in Theological Interpretation series. I have become convinced that certain accounts wishing to place the responsibility for canon formation in the church are rightly concerned with certain problematical North American formulations of *sola scriptura* and inspiration. This has led to an appeal to church authority and the rule of faith from an otherwise unlikely quarter. But the threat to the formative place of the Old Testament and its influence on the New Testament is often subsumed into theories of an open canon, Scripture rather than canon, and now a rule of faith whose scriptural rootage and grounding are obscured. The reader will see in the present work aspects of that concern, even as the present project sees the issue from the standpoint of standard accounts of the canon and debates about the status of the Old Testament at the time of the New Testament. The other project, titled *The Character of Christian Scripture*, addresses the issue from the standpoint of a two-Testament scriptural legacy and how the church should handle that canonical form in its present life.

My present concern is to understand the unique character of the prophetic division of the scriptures of Israel. Work on the book of the Twelve Minor Prophets has affected an older discussion about canon formation, and that new and exciting work has yet to find its place in discussions respecting the canon. I hope the present work remedies that and turns the discussion in a more theological and hermeneutical direction.

I am grateful for a series of conversations and thesis-topic discussions on canon and the Writings with Amber Warhurst and Timothy Stone, PhD students at St. Andrews. They have thought carefully about key issues in respect of canon. Mark Elliott, Daniel Driver, Mark Gignilliat, Nathan MacDonald, and others read portions of the manuscript and offered helpful comments. Steve Chapman at Duke has published his own trenchant analysis of canon, and he pointed me to several recent works. Georg Steins of Osnabrück gave an insightful lecture on canon at the 2007 Society of Biblical Literature international meeting in Vienna and was kind enough to send me his manuscript. Too late for me to incorporate was the 2005 Lund dissertation of Tomas Bokedal, a review of which has appeared in the October 2007 issue of *Journal of Theological Studies*.

While I was preparing these talks and reflecting on matters of canon and the Twelve, my close friend and colleague Brevard Childs had a fall upon returning from the United Kingdom that led to serious complications and, sadly and tragically, his untimely death. I cannot begin to express my gratitude for everything this great and kind man taught me, in seminar room, parlor, pulpit, and pew. The loss of his companionship and counsel is inestimable. I have had the opportunity to read his (now to be published posthumously) manuscript on the Pauline Letters, and it is a stunning, clear, and morally urgent series of reflections. The implications of canon formation are deeply imbedded in the processes of the Bible's coming to be and do not exist as extrinsic maneuvers in subsequent communities seeking to understand themselves or address perceived needs. The canon emerges from the lived life of Israel under the word of God, faithfully straining to hear that word and obey and live. The church's role in canon is that of gratefully acknowledging a witness prepared in prophet and apostle and seeking to honor the providential work of God in Christ from within their own distinctive providential location.

My conviction is that the book of the Twelve is a "goodly fellowship of the Prophets," akin to the apostolic fellowship represented by the Pauline Letter Collection within the canonical New Testament, and likely influencing both its formation and form. The book of the Twelve shows a sophisticated composition intended to preserve the historicality of God's word vouchsafed to individual prophets and to address the generations beyond their times, which come to the Twelve to learn from the past so as to find present obedient hope and direction.

The present work is dedicated to Brevard Childs and his wife, Ann. This seems a meager offering, I must say, given all that Bard has taught me and the wider world, and in light of many years of friendship and collaboration of various kinds. But I trust in the end that all God has said through him will remain a legacy for generations to come and its own kind of canonical witness, appropriate to the place God set him down in his mercy and loving-kindness. We have Ann to thank for so many things, and I am grateful that she remains a witness to Bard and his work and to the God who inspires us all in his service and in his hope.

Christopher Seitz

Abbreviations

BHS	*Biblia Hebraica Stuttgartensia*, ed. K. Elliger and W. Rudolph (Stuttgart: Deutsche Bibelgesellschaft, 1967–77)
BZAW	Beihefte zur Zeitschrift für die alttestamentliche Wissenschaft
DtrH	Deuteronomistic history
FAT	Forschungen zum Alten Testament
JR	*Journal of Religion*
JSOT	*Journal for the Study of the Old Testament*
JSOTSup	Journal for the Study of the Old Testament: Supplement Series
MT	Masoretic Text
NICOT	New International Commentary on the Old Testament
NT	New Testament
NV	*Nova et vetera*
OBT	Overtures to Biblical Theology
OT	Old Testament

OTL	Old Testament Library
ProEccl	*Pro ecclesia*
SBLSymS	Society of Biblical Literature Symposium Series
SJT	*Scottish Journal of Theology*
STI	Studies in Theological Interpretation
TynBul	*Tyndale Bulletin*

Introduction

Canon and the Goodly Fellowship of the Prophets

The glorious company of the Apostles praise thee.
The goodly fellowship of the Prophets praise thee.
The noble army of Martyrs praise thee.
The holy Church throughout all the world doth ac-
    knowledge thee;
the Father, of an infinite majesty;
thine adorable, true, and only Son;
also the Holy Ghost, the Comforter.
Thou art the King of Glory, O Christ.
Thou art the everlasting Son of the Father.

—Te Deum, Book of Common Prayer

The Fate of the Old Testament in Canon Discussions

In an essay that appeared the year before his untimely death, Brevard Childs noted that recent discussions of canon went in different directions in North American and Continental publications.[1] Doubtless this reflects cultural and ecclesial differences of the kind Childs noted in 1970 in *Biblical Theology in Crisis*. In that book, he showed how confusing and ill suited were methods developed in Lutheran and Reformed circles in Europe when they migrated into the life of Protestant churches and their institutions in North America. The theological context of critical methods was not sufficiently grasped and often did not match the concern with empiricism and evidentialism of greater importance in North American discussions.[2]

In the later essay, the topic was more specifically canon and Childs's contributions to that, in a series of landmark publications appearing in the decades following *Biblical Theology in Crisis*. Europeans were interested for the most part in Childs's work on canon from the standpoint of biblical theology and older questions of the relation of the Testaments, as well as newer concerns with reception history (or *Wirkungsgeschichte*), Jesus Christ and the OT, Israel and church, and so forth. North Americans, by contrast, focused on material issues, influenced by the discoveries at the Dead Sea and kindred finds. Here the concern was with closure, selection, exclusion, and delimitation. Reception history was a factor only to the degree that it was a resource for helping with these questions by supplying lists of the biblical books, citations, and clues as to the status of the canon. Canon, on these terms, was unable to work as a theological and

1. Brevard Childs, "The Canon in Recent Biblical Studies: Reflections on an Era," *ProEccl* 14 (2005): 26–45. The essay is reprinted as the lead chapter in C. Bartholomew et al., eds., *Canon and Biblical Interpretation* (Milton Keynes, UK: Paternoster; Grand Rapids: Zondervan, 2006).

2. Brevard Childs, *Biblical Theology in Crisis* (Philadelphia: Westminster, 1970). On the problems of empirical referentiality and the "God who acts," see L. Gilkey, "Cosmology, Ontology, and the Travail of Biblical Language," *JR* 41 (1961): 194–205.

hermeneutical index since it was delimited to formal matters of closure and institutional decisions—which might in their own way call for reconsideration, depending on the predispositions of the interpreter (consider the work of Helmut Koester or Bart Ehrman). Only here would the hermeneutical dimension intrude.

Lately, a new dimension has emerged to breathe a kind of hermeneutical life into these more formal descriptions of canon. Lee McDonald, for example, has popularized old standards of canon development and closure traceable to Albert Sundberg. These old theories are left pretty much untouched, in spite of the discussions Childs has noted taking place on the Continent, with which there is little if any exchange. How might one use these theories hermeneutically? James Sanders had earlier put forward his own species of what he called "canon criticism" in an effort to describe the Bible as a resource for a form of reader-response application. The canon, as he saw it, was a collection of competing and dialogical voices. This view turned away from the details of closure and the assessment of that after the fact from the side of hermeneutics. Rather, it liked the idea of process and earlier development and saw in it the potential to link up with adaptability and diversity as hermeneutically rich concepts. The canon was a container. Nothing about its given form was crucial except to the degree that it preserved multiple voices and offered clues to motivations and identity struggles and so forth. Canon was a tribute to conversation inside Scripture. Picking up an older romantic notion of experiential-expressivist identification, it was a relatively straightforward move to see canon as a subset of this conception. People in the Bible had conversations and dialogues with one another over important religious issues, and so do we. In the light of the first reality, the second finds warrant and its own kind of dialogue partner. This is the genius of canon. Sanders also believed his material descriptions of canon matched up with the more hermeneutical dimension.[3]

In McDonald one sees a slightly different marriage of concern with material matters of closure and listing with hermeneutics and application. When one succeeds in seeing stability and theological significance in the OT only in old subsections (i.e., Torah; the remaining books are diverse religious literature), it releases the wider scriptural canon from a role of authoritative influence on the formation of the NT and on basic Christian witness, including such a role for the work and person of Jesus Christ. Canon, on these terms, becomes "scripture," which in turn is a loose collection of religious writings.

Perhaps unexpectedly, this excusing of the OT from a central significance in early canon formation leaves the role to be occupied by the church (or "community of faith"). The church forms the NT canon according to principles reconstructed by the interpreter (be they Weber/Marxist or anti-Warfield), and the OT comes along after the fact, now in its guise as diverse religious writings.[4] On this model, the

3. J. Sanders, "Adaptable for Life: The Nature and Function of Canon," in *Magnalia Dei: The Mighty Acts of God; Essays on the Bible and Archeology in Memory of G. E. Wright* (New York: Doubleday, 1976), 531–60. For further bibliography, see the discussion to follow.

4. On terms congenial with the work of Barton and McDonald, C. Allert puts a question in a form that seems quite natural to him, given his understanding of the Scriptures of Israel: "How and why did the church come to accept as authoritative Scripture a NT containing no more and no less than twenty-seven books, and *to place this alongside either the Hebrew or the Greek Scriptures, renamed the 'Old Testament'*?" (C. D. Allert, *A High View of Scripture? The Authority of the Bible and the Formation of the New Testament Canon*, Evangelical *Ressourcement* [Grand Rapids: Baker Academic, 2007], 41, emphasis mine). The foundational role of the Scriptures (Law and Prophets) for the logic of the rule of faith is overlooked entirely in this conceptuality.

scriptures of Israel become what the theory believed in the first place: general religious background material in the history of religion or, trading on a German Lutheran model, a tradition-historical development leading up to the NT. In McDonald's hands, now followed by Craig Allert, recourse is to be had to a rule of faith, as they understand this.[5] That is, given the more evangelically orientated context of their own work, the discussion shifts to address the front occupied by accounts of the Bible that stress inspiration and inerrancy. In an effort to replace this Anglo-Saxon view of *sola scriptura* as it exists within North American evangelicalism and a NT canon that gives rise to the church, McDonald and Allert seek to dethrone what the latter calls a "high view of Scripture" by calling on the Christian assembly to define the limits of the NT canon. This is done by appeal to what they call "the rule of faith."[6]

5. L. McDonald, "Identifying Scripture and Canon in the Early Church: The Criteria Question," in *The Canon Debate*, L. McDonald and J. Sanders (Peabody, MA: Hendrickson, 2002), 416–39. In the introduction, he speaks of the "Bible as dialogical literature" and of "efforts to resolve the tension made by such an observation" as leading to appeals to canon within a canon and other such lenses (ibid., 15). He also mentions a rule of faith: "Some suggest reliance on an abstracted or even external *regula fidei* ('rule of faith') by which to guide the perplexed" (ibid.). The *regula fidei* within the early church, it is to be argued here, is intrinsic to how Scripture makes its larger Christian claims felt, based on a grasp of the plain sense of the OT Scripture in the light of Christ's according work.

6. Allert describes the rule as entailing "a progression of thought that moves from the teaching of Jesus, who hands it over to his apostles, who subsequently pass it on to the church, which is then charged with guarding the pure teaching" (*High View*, 54). This is unobjectionable except that Jesus is not known apart from scriptural promise and accordance, and the rule is the means of asserting this fact. There is no "progression" that is not essentially accordance, deference, and confirmation of the claims of a scriptural inheritance. One cannot remove the matter of a "scriptural Jesus" (in accordance with the testimony declaring his relationship to the God who sent him and with whom he is one) from a discussion of the canon of the NT, formed with this confession at its center. This is the rule of faith's logic in the ante-Nicene fathers. See my discussion in *The Character of Christian Scripture: Canon and the Rule of Faith* (Grand Rapids: Baker Academic, forthcoming). "We must remember that by 'Scripture' the Fathers, up to Irenaeus,

It should probably not be surprising that having eliminated the canon of the OT from any significant hermeneutical and theological role in the formation of the NT, they also fail to comprehend the scriptures of Israel as the key to understanding the rule of faith in the period in question. Instead, the rule of faith becomes a vague descriptor for something like "central apostolic teaching," which in turn serves as a criterion for canonical decisions with respect to the NT. Not only does this criterion jump the fence wherein the usual descriptions of the rule of faith are sought by scholars surveying the ante-Nicene fathers and their appeal to the rule. These descriptions also see the rule as the exegetical grounding of

Hippolytus, and Theophilus of Antioch, usually meant the Old Testament. At first this was the only approved and recommended collection of writings. But the *paradosis* of the Church, faithful to that of the apostles, was precisely this transmission of the Christ-event, as based documentarily on the Old Testament writings and, at the same time, explaining the meaning of these writings" (Yves Congar, *Tradition and Traditions* [London: Burns & Oates, 1966], 31). "In the Christian faith from the very first both elements, Jesus and the Scripture, were mutually and inseparably related" (Hans von Campenhausen, *The Formation of the Christian Bible* [London: Adam & Charles Black, 1972], 21). "There is, of course, no need to argue the authority or the extent of the Old Testament, for the Old Testament canon was in practice an already long established fact. For the NT books it is different" (E. Flesseman-Van Leer, *Tradition and Scripture in the Early Church* [Assen: Van Gorcum, 1954], 131). On the centrality of the older Scriptures for demonstrating Christ, Behr notes: "Although Irenaeus clearly knows the apostolic writings [en route to a NT canon], the substance of his exposition is drawn exclusively from Scripture: that Jesus was born of a virgin and worked miracles is shown from Isaiah and others; while the names of Pilate and Herod are known from the evangelists, that Christ was bound and brought before them is shown by Hosea; that he was crucified, raised and exalted is again shown by the prophets. In the first part of the work ([*Demonstration*] 3b–42a), Irenaeus recounts the scriptural history of God's salvific work which culminates in the apostolic proclamation of Christ. In the second part of the work (4b–97), Irenaeus demonstrates how all the things which have come to pass in Jesus Christ, were spoken by the prophets, both so that we might believe in God, as what he previously proclaimed has come to pass, and also to demonstrate that Scripture throughout does in fact speak of Jesus Christ, the Word of God, as preached by the apostles" (John Behr, *The Formation of Christian Theology*, vol. 1, *The Way to Nicaea* [Crestwood, NY: St. Vladimir's Seminary Press, 2001], 30).

basic theological affirmation in the scriptures of Israel—that is, that Jesus Christ the Son, or Logos, and the Creator God of Israel, the maker of heaven and earth, YHWH, are one. In addition, they understand the formation of the NT as dependent on a criterion that must be conjectured as fundamental to canonical decisions in respect of the NT (the rule of faith) as against the usual ones of apostolicity, catholicity, and so on. Again, this is probably consistent with the view that the "canon" of the OT is a development external to itself and trades on decisions tied up with the canonicity of the NT. Without understanding the rule of faith as operating in conjunction with a scriptural witness from Israel, they give it a role suitable to the churchly determinations with respect to the NT. The evidence of the early church and modern patristic studies of the role of the OT in the rule of faith has been insufficiently assessed and integrated. This has apparently happened out of a concern that the church has been insufficiently appreciated by evangelical North Americans as an ingredient in the formation of the NT. It would be a sad consequence of this if the crucial role of the OT in the early church were evacuated.

Recent Work on the Twelve and the Character of the Prophetic Accomplishment

One distinguishing feature of the present work is the incorporation of recent analysis of the book of the Twelve. Consolidation of the Twelve did not happen after the fact in terms of external editing, shuffling, exclusion, and closure but belongs intrinsically to the prophetic accomplishment of the Twelve itself. In the earliest phases we can detect, interest in relating individual witnesses to one another is evident. This is motivated by a desire to show how the one God of Israel is speaking in mutually influencing ways through historically discrete figures. Because this conception has a counterpart in the book of Isaiah (over the long history of its development) and because it also is related to the history of the prophetic word seen in the Joshua–2 Kings complex (the so-called Deuteronomistic history), it is appropriate to let these findings of historical and canonical analysis have their impact on the older discussions of canon and the formation of the OT in that process.

In his first foray into the field of canon studies,[7] Lee McDonald cites with approval the older view of James Barr, going back to Albert Sundberg, that NT references "strongly suggest that the category of 'Prophet' was not a closed one: any non-Torah book that was holy scripture was a 'Prophet.'"[8] This view trades in part on the idea that the canon develops one section at a time, rather than in mutually influencing and reinforcing ways, and also that the achievement of the Prophets is a kind of secondary sifting of all non-Mosaic books. This led to the determination of a category such as "Writings," in one context, and to categories such as history books, prophetic books, lyrical books, and so on in another. By speaking of the non-Mosaic books as a random collection, a particular construal of the evidence is made possible, and a dampening down of the idea of a distinctive prophetic accomplishment results.[9] Ironically, it is

7. L. McDonald, *The Formation of the Christian Biblical Canon* (Nashville: Abingdon, 1988), 53.
8. J. Barr, *Holy Scripture: Canon, Authority, Criticism* (Philadelphia: Westminster, 1983), 55.
9. Allert can make this kind of statement, reflecting the confusion: "The early Christians did not divide the Hebrew Scriptures the way the Jews did" (*High View*, 46), that is, according to the Law, Prophets, Writings division. This is an inaccurate and oversimplified statement of the matter. It also gives the impression that there

precisely the hard work of the historical-critical method that best points to this accomplishment happening within Israel and not at later times due to the significant methodological and theological reflections on large-scale endeavors such as the Deuteronomistic history, Isaiah as a sixty-six-chapter work, and now the book of the Twelve. In the view of the present book, this hard work has not been adequately incorporated. The idea of a random collection of non-Mosaic books is a legacy of the stages-of-canonicity conception, which must ignore the sophisticated character of large-scale collections such as the Deuteronomistic history, the book of the Twelve, Isaiah, and the combination and mutual influence of these works on one another at the compositional level. The chronological argument never worked well with respect to the Writings, some of which are earlier than the prophetic books and nevertheless were not merged into these compositional accomplishments.

McDonald continues with a further reference to Barr's theory: "Although Barr agrees that the Law was a separate and distinct part of the Jewish canon, he maintains that the boundaries among the Prophets and the other books were still imprecise even in the first century CE." Then McDonald adverts that, at least for some Jews in the earlier period, a distinction existed and the Prophets were "more precise."[10]

In a later edition of this work, he then adds this view of the matter: "While we do not object to the view that the Former (or Early) Prophets (Joshua, Judges, Samuels, and Kings) had most likely been collected and circulated with the books of Moses in the late sixth to early fifth century BCE, it

are "Christians" over here and "Jews" over there, each with their own "Bible" by the period of Barnabas.

10. McDonald, *Formation*, 53.

is another matter to say that they were recognized as sacred
scripture on par with the law of Moses."[11] This conception
is flawed at several points. First, the "Former Prophets" do
not seek a parity or grade of acceptance with the Law. Their
relationship to Law is reciprocal.[12] So the idea of being "on
par" bespeaks the faulty (additive) model he envisages. Second, apparently trading on a view of Sanders,[13] he refers to
a "Genesis to Kings complex." But this ignores the accomplishment of the Deuteronomistic history in relationship to
Torah, which resulted not in a continuous historical narrative
but in a grammar of Law and Prophets.[14]

Failure to understand the significance of this conjunction,
which led to Deuteronomy's key hermeneutical position at the
close of the Pentateuch, leads then to a further confusion.[15]
McDonald continues the quote above with this comment: "It
is even less likely that the Latter Prophets (Isaiah, Jeremiah,
Ezekiel, Daniel and the Twelve) had obtained such a position

11. L. McDonald, *The Formation of the Christian Biblical Canon*, rev. and
expanded ed. (Peabody, MA: Hendrickson, 1995), 31.
12. S. Chapman, *The Law and the Prophets: A Study in Old Testament Canon
Formation*, FAT 27 (Tübingen: Mohr Siebeck, 2000).
13. J. Sanders, *Torah and Canon* (Philadelphia: Fortress, 1972), 91.
14. On the problems with such a view in the magisterial work of von Rad,
see C. Seitz, *Prophecy and Hermeneutics: Toward a New Introduction to the
Prophets*, STI (Grand Rapids: Baker Academic, 2007); and R. Rendtorff, *Canon
and Theology: Overtures to an Old Testament Theology*, OBT (Minneapolis:
Fortress, 1993).
15. In an unpublished paper read at the 2007 international meeting of the
Society of Biblical Literature in Vienna, Georg Steins argues along the lines of the
present work. About the Torah-Prophets complex (of the present MT order and
arrangement), he states that there is no canonized Torah without Prophets, for a
Torah without interpretation is inconceivable ("Es gibt keine kanonisierte Tora
ohne Nebiim, da eine 'Tora' ohne Auslegung nicht vorstellbar ist"; p. 13). He also
envisions what he calls a hybrid formation ("Gestaltung von zweierlei Herkunft")
consisting of the Torah-Prophets achievement on one side and a different Ketubim
conceptuality and canonical formation ("Zwei Konzepte—ein Kanon: Zur Gestalt
und Gestaltung des TaNaK"). This is an important contribution to the discussion.
He also provides a careful assessment of work by Albert de Pury (on the Writings),
Stephen Chapman, and Karel van der Toorn.

(being 'on par') among the Jews by that time."[16] Several things can again be noted in this flawed conception. First, McDonald tips his hand here and in the handling of the "Former Prophets" when he reflexively speaks of them as a species of continuous history, distinguishing them from the Prophets as such and then including Daniel in the number of the latter. This replicates decisions made in certain translated forms of the OT and indicates the way his mind is working. The achievement of the Deuteronomistic history—intrinsic to the development of the OT within its own historical context—is ignored in favor of a much later rearrangement known in certain forms of the Greek Bible. One gets a sense then that the "Latter Prophets" (he does not use the term, but instead gives a familiar English Bible list) are distinct from the Former Prophets, when the achievement of early canon formation was precisely to level any distinction between them in the name of creating a complex category of non-Mosaic books with their own character.

The historical reality is that already at Qumran one can see the book of the Twelve as a single, ordered collection.[17] Recent historical-critical work has shown how massive is the accomplishment of this Twelve-Book collection. The fact that two major *collections* of works existed deep within the historical life of Israel indicates that efforts to describe the "canon" or "Scriptures" at the time of the NT as consisting of a stable Torah conjoined in some sense with a random enumeration of individual works ("a diverse collection of religious works with definite bounds") has seriously misread the evidence. One can add here as well the newer work on Isaiah, which

16. McDonald, *Formation* (rev. ed.), 31.
17. See the recent, thorough evaluation of Dead Sea Scroll manuscripts of the Twelve by F. Watson in *Paul and the Hermeneutics of Faith* (Edinburgh: T&T Clark, 2004), 78–88.

sees the sixty-six-chapter book coming together as a result
of intentional and highly sophisticated labor ("a canonical
process of shaping") stretching over the same time frame and
addressing the same series of generations as the Twelve. The
point is that the "goodly fellowship of the Prophets" is its own
special achievement. The Deuteronomistic history provides an
account of the divine word spoken by key prophetic figures
and by "all my servants the prophets" (Jer. 7:25) through the
history from Joshua to the exile, and the superscriptions of
the Three Major Prophets and the Twelve clearly intend us
to read the witness of the individual prophetic works in the
light of the Prophetic History, and vice versa. To put the
development of a prophetic canon (including Daniel) down
to postexilic concerns for identity[18] is badly to misconstrue
the concern for coordinating the one divine word spoken by
different prophets, a concern traceable to the formation of
the very first prophetic works of Amos and Hosea.[19]

According to this view, it matters little whether the final
dating of these related editorial processes can be sharply distinguished, a theory that is questionable in its own right. Mc-
Donald appears to believe that a completed Deuteronomistic
history existed prior to the other prophetic books in a way
that makes it "more canonical" because of this, in contrast
to the Three and the Twelve. But the evidence is rather that
these great complexes of prophetic narrative and prophetic
books are intimately related (consider the cross-references
and major associations linking Micah and Isaiah, Micah

18. McDonald here cites with approval Sanders, *Torah and Canon*, 91.
19. See the very penetrating essay of J. Jeremias, "The Interrelationship between Amos and Hosea," in *Forming Prophetic Literature: Essays on Isaiah and
the Twelve in Honor of John D. W. Watts*, ed. James W. Watts and Paul R. House,
JSOTSup 235 (Sheffield: Sheffield Academic Press, 1996), 171–86; and my discussion in *Prophecy and Hermeneutics*.

and Jeremiah, Isaiah and Kings, Obadiah and Jeremiah, and Jeremiah and Kings). It is of course counter-intuitive to think of Amos functioning in any form only after the "historical" Former Prophets' consolidation. Newer work on the Twelve is instrumental in this debate because it shows how integrative were the concerns that brought about the accomplishment of this prophetic collection. These are traceable to the beginning of the process and are not additive features from a later period. Here again, the logic of sequential historical development (one-after-the-other closing phases), wrongly applied to Torah and Former Prophets, has been wrongly argued in the case of the prophetic accomplishment itself.

Conclusions

In what follows, we introduce the matter of canonicity and seek to relate it to newer developments in critical assessments of the Prophets. It will be our argument that the Writings do not seek a character of internal association akin to what we see in the Prophetic subdivision, and never did. They are a library of books whose associations are extrinsic to the books of the Torah-Prophets collection. This collection is the key grammar of the OT, reckoning with a lineage of prophecy begun with Moses and extended in History and individual Prophetic collections until Malachi and the hope for a "messenger" like him—one who will prepare the generation to whom he appears in the manner of Malachi himself in the context of the day of the Lord and in the light of intimations of this day in the book of the Twelve. This conception of prophecy is integrally related to Torah, that foundational account of God's instruction, but also chiefly to God's character, which is fundamental to any understanding of the thrust of the book of the Twelve. "The LORD, compassionate and merciful, slow to anger . . . but who will by no means clear the guilty" (cf. Exod. 34:6–7) is the main "theme" of the book of the Twelve, introduced in Hosea and serving as the source of hope and of justice in the context of affairs in the northern and southern kingdoms, in the nations, and in the remnant community of the final prophets Haggai, Zechariah, and Malachi. The efforts at associating and grounding this larger movement of the Twelve with Isaiah, Jeremiah, and Ezekiel and with the prophetic history are prodigious and inspiring.

Turning this "achievement of association" into a collection of any non-Mosaic book, blurs the character of both the Prophets and the Writings. That in subsequent lists and arrangements the Writings may migrate is only an indication of logical movements or innocent changes that seek to make sense of associations operating extrinsically, true to the character of the Writings as Writings. It is meaningful to speak of an "open canon," if by that is meant the capacity of the Law and the Prophets to function as canon, no matter the precise number or order of the books in the third distinctive section. Subsequent rearrangements are not so much the consequence of decisions to create rival orders as they are introductions of patterns of migration whose logic is patient of explanation. To use this phenomenon to argue for a distinction between Scripture and canon not only confuses the issue but also renders the significance of the core canon of Law and Prophets, as the NT acknowledges and defers to this, muddled and imprecise as an authoritative witness fundamental in the formation of the NT and in the early church's appeal to a rule of faith.

1

Starting Points

If they do not hear Moses and the prophets, neither will they be convinced if some one should rise from the dead.

Luke 16:31 RSV

This is one of the most remarkable passages in the NT. It speaks of the sufficiency of the scriptures of Israel to accomplish what even a resurrection from the dead cannot improve upon. It is spoken by one who will return from the dead and who as his first act will open these same scriptures and show himself to be teacher, main theme, and final end, the subject matter (*res*) of the scriptures of Israel.

Our concern in these chapters is related to this key passage yet takes as its wider point of departure the specific question of the material form of the scriptures of Israel at the time of the formation of the NT. Some have argued that reference to "the Law and the Prophets" in the NT means that the third section of the canon, the division otherwise referred to as "the Writings," was not yet stable. Luke's later reference to Moses, the Prophets, and the Psalms is regarded as confirming rather than contradicting this point (Luke 24:44). According to this view, reference to Psalms alone indicates that the third section is still a vague grouping. A variation of this view holds that the phrase "the Law and the Prophets" means that the Law of Moses was stable, that all other books were called prophetic, and that a tripartite division was not yet in force. Moreover, the non-Mosaic books are viewed as diverse, without fixed sequence, open in scope, and inclusive of other books. "A wide religious literature without definite bounds" is the way one scholar put it.[1] The determination of the OT canon, such as it was, was not made until some time after the NT and was caught up in the selfsame struggle of the NT to achieve its own canonical status, ordered shape, and a logic of authority and apostolicity.[2]

This popular reconstruction is faulty at key points. First, it misunderstands *the unique achievement of the prophetic division of the canon* as a division different in kind from the Law or the Writings. This makes the idea of a coherent Mosaic grouping and a different, diverse, unstructured second grouping improbable. Second, such a view makes *closure the*

1. A. Sundberg, *The Old Testament of the Early Christian Church* (Cambridge, MA: Harvard University Press, 1964), 102.
2. J. Barton, *The Spirit and the Letter: Studies in the Biblical Canon* (London: SPCK, 1997); idem, *Holy Writings, Sacred Texts: The Canon in Early Christianity* (London: SPCK, 1997); idem, *The Making of the Christian Bible* (London: Darton, Longman & Todd, 1997); idem, *The Old Testament: Canon, Literature, and Theology* (Aldershot: Ashgate, 2007); James Barr, *Holy Scripture: Canon, Authority, Criticism* (Philadelphia: Westminster, 1983); L. McDonald and J. Sanders, eds., *The Canon Debate* (Peabody, MA: Hendrickson, 2002); C. D. Allert, *A High View of Scripture? The Authority of the Bible and the Formation of the New Testament Canon*, Evangelical *Ressourcement* (Grand Rapids: Baker Academic, 2007).

most fundamental aspect of canonical authority when there are other ways of considering canon as a key feature of the scriptures of Israel. The Law and the Prophets, I shall argue, is a grammar—that is, this literary conjunction is the means (rule and syntax) by which the language of Israel's scriptures makes its voice most fundamentally heard, and hearing that rightly is unaffected by the existence of additional writings. Third, the Writings as individual works assume and operate in relationship to this grammar, and their precise number and order are not crucial on the same terms. The actual character of the Writings must be properly grasped if the issue of closure and scope is to be understood.

Finally, I shall argue that the popular reconstruction misunderstands two features at work in the Law and the Prophets as the grammar of Israel's scriptural inheritance. First, the formation of the NT has been affected by the OT, not simply in the area of intellectual or religious background[3] or in the area of citation and subsequent usage, an area critical for key NT convictions as well as for the church's understanding of how the OT might be used exegetically following Paul.[4] Rather, the grouping of the Law and the Prophets, in its ordered form, provides key categories of hermeneutics and

3. The work of N. T. Wright relies heavily on this conception. The OT serves as a resource from which to gather ideas and religious conceptions that are operative, as Wright reconstructs this, at the period of the earthly Jesus, informing his mission, stipulating a theory of history with exile in prominence, and so forth. See my evaluation in "Reconciliation and the Plain Sense Witness of Scripture," in *The Redemption: An Interdisciplinary Symposium on Christ as Redeemer*, ed. S. T. Davis, D. Kendall, and G. O'Collins (Oxford: Oxford University Press, 2004), 25–42.

4. Richard Hays and Francis Watson are representative of such a view. See R. Hays, *Echoes of Scripture in the Letters of Paul* (New Haven: Yale University Press, 1989); F. Watson, *Paul and the Hermeneutics of Faith* (Edinburgh: T&T Clark, 2004). See the fuller discussion in C. Seitz, *The Character of Christian Scripture*, STI (Grand Rapids: Baker Academic, forthcoming).

re-application, of affiliation and association, critical for the formation of the NT and for our understanding of the NT as canon. Appreciation of these categories is essential if we are to understand the implications of the NT's canonical form, especially in the fourfold Gospel collection, Acts (and its separation from Luke), and the diverse collection of Pauline Letters and Catholic Epistles.

The influence of the OT's canonical form on the NT's canonical form has not been noted in sufficient detail, if at all. In part this is because until recently the OT's canonical form has not been the subject of extended treatments and also because those who do appreciate this aspect fail to register its significance for a proper understanding of theology and hermeneutics in the NT and in biblical theology more generally. Watson's *Paul and the Hermeneutics of Faith* is a case in point. The constraining and interpreting character of the canonical form of the OT is crucial in Watson's account, but these same considerations fall out when it comes to interpretation of the NT.[5] The OT is read canonically; the NT is read according to a historical reconstruction of the intentions of Paul on key matters of justification by faith or the "second use" (theological use) of the law. This leads, in my view, to a truncated or partial understanding of both the OT and the NT when it comes to the law, a proper theological

5. In order to understand the "intention" of Habakkuk in his statement "the righteous shall live by his faith" (2:4), one must allow Habakkuk to function within the larger movement of the book of the Twelve. Paul has rightly heard Habakkuk, according to this appreciation of the canonical shape of the OT. In the case of the Law, however, Watson tracks far less closely the actual final form of the books of the Pentateuch, where one could find all three "uses" of the law, because he is interested in the "second use." This does not reflect the total canonical witness of the OT, and it isolates only one perspective on law in the canonical NT. This is the fallout from a model that focuses on single authorial intention in the NT while attending (in better and in worse ways) to the canonical intention of the OT.

understanding of which requires a grasp of the totality of the NT witness and not just this or that individual witness. Such a reconstruction can be exacerbated by linking an individual reconstruction of the intentions of Paul to an alleged "canonical reading" of selected portions of the Pentateuch.

There is a further aspect at stake. In the early church, appeal is made to the rule of faith. Central to understanding the rule is the *evolving character of the NT canon* and the need in such a period to have recourse to a stable witness that lays out the basic grammar of the God of Israel and his people. The Law and the Prophets—to be called the OT when the NT comes to form—was viewed as a privileged, stable witness against which the claims of the gospel were tested and shown to have been established from of old. This theological conviction (Christ at work in creation and in Israel) was a distinctive Christian accomplishment, but it was made on the basis of a stable witness whose sense was taken to be both plain and figural. The rule establishes the providential work of God in Christ, in creation, in the promise to the patriarchs, in the word spoken in Law and Prophet, in prediction, type, and moral example (for a classic account, see Irenaeus's *Demonstration of the Apostolic Preaching*). An account of the Law and the Prophets that emphasizes diversity, lack of closure, and no ordered form fails properly to assess the appeal to the rule of faith and its implications for a Christian canon in the making. The NT takes form and derives its authority not only with respect to apostolic memory or eyewitnessing (as a fresh account now has it).[6] Crucial for the formation of the NT and its canonical logic

6. R. Bauckham, *Jesus and the Eyewitnesses* (Grand Rapids: Eerdmans, 2006). See my essay "Accordance: The Scriptures of Israel as Eyewitness," *NV* 6 (2008): 513–22.

is a proper understanding of the Law and the Prophets upon which this logic is based in the confession of Jesus Christ as Son of God in accordance with the Scriptures.

Those who believe that the OT's canonical character is intimately tied up with that of the NT are correct, but they have the influence running in the wrong direction. The OT does not accomplish a canonical authority in the context of churchly reflections on a rule of faith or in the debates and evolving consensus about the way the NT may properly be received as canon in a fixed form. The OT's canonical form and status are the assisting means by which a collateral apostolic witness emerges and finds its structure and authority. The rule of faith is that appeal to the christological and (incipiently) trinitarian claims of the OT, such as we find these in the accordance statements of the evolving traditions of the apostolic writings, en route to becoming a NT.[7]

Two images may help explain what is at stake. The first concerns two bridges. In Charleston, South Carolina, stretching over the wide Cooper River, was a remarkable steel bridge. It was high enough to accommodate great shipping vessels, and it had to gain its height very quickly, rising as it did from sea level. The Cooper River Bridge eventually had to be replaced. A massive new structure was conceived, with its starting point on the north side of the river now placed at a considerable distance back and joined into the interstate highway system. While the new bridge was under construction, the old bridge continued to do its work. The new bridge slowly took form

7. See John Behr, *The Formation of Christian Theology*, vol. 1, *The Way to Nicaea* (Crestwood, NY: St. Vladimir's Seminary Press, 2001). For a good example of the accordance logic as it surfaces in the NT, see: "For I delivered to you as of first importance what I also received, that Christ died for our sins in accordance with the scriptures, that he was buried, that he was raised on the third day in accordance with the scriptures . . . " (1 Cor. 15:3 RSV).

with respect to the old bridge, towering over it and eventually dwarfing it, showing it to be clearly the bridge of a former day. The supports for the new bridge were placed with reference to the old. When the new bridge was finished, the old was allowed to fall into the river, section by section until all was done. Anyone who recalls the old bridge knows how influential it was in forming the new bridge. In theory, the old bridge could have been retained, and traffic allowed to use it, perhaps for special events. But its chief use was for traffic from an older day and for help in constructing a new bridge. Those with special awareness of engineering emphasized the indispensability of the old bridge, and tribute to it was not without its special character. Occasionally, one heard that the old bridge was an eyesore, dangerous, and always in need of demolition, but these voices were not major ones.[8]

A more appropriate way to understand the old bridge, or the OT, would not have been to leave it standing; for the basic analogy is faulty to begin with.

A second image suggests itself. One may think that there is an allergy to things old when compared to newer models (a legacy of the consumer West).[9] There are exceptions to this

8. See the discussion of Barnabas in Brevard Childs's analysis of Hebrews within the NT canon (*Biblical Theology of the Old and New Testaments: Theological Reflection on the Christian Bible* [Minneapolis: Fortress, 1992], 312–13).

9. Gerald Bray speaks of the reverse instinct at the time of the early church. He describes the church fathers as being aware of the great monuments and as believing antiquity was a more impressive age than their own ("The Church Fathers and Biblical Theology," in *Out of Egypt: Biblical Theology and Biblical Interpretation* [Milton Keynes, UK: Paternoster; Grand Rapids: Zondervan, 2004], 31). Bray writes, "A third-century Alexandrian like Origen would have known about the pyramids of ancient Egypt, but he would not have seen anything of comparable magnificence being built in his own day, and he would probably have sensed that the skills needed for pyramid building had been lost over the course of time. The Bible, after all, told him that in ancient times people lived far longer than they do now—something that pointed to historical decline rather than to progress. We forget it now, but it was not until about 1800 that people began to think of

tendency, of course: old, historic golf courses; Ivy League
schools; single malt scotch; and so on. Here "old" is good.
If people were required to walk on their knees to play golf at
the Old Course in St. Andrews, they would. If you told them
they could play the New Course (a nineteenth-century links
course), even if it might be more challenging, they would
demur. Unsurprisingly, the Old Course is now actually too
short, given its age and the space-age equipment now used to
launch high-tech golf balls, but adjustments have been made.
The tee boxes are placed as far back as possible, sometimes
on adjacent links. Soon, one will putt out and then have to
walk back half the length of the previous fairway in order
to find the next tee box.

The point of this second analogy is as follows: What is
new, for the purposes of playing the same game at a later
time under new circumstances, must take its bearings with
reference to what is old, or one is not really participating
according to the desired terms. Here the concern is with *incorporation within the original game* for outsiders who are
temporally and even "religiously" distant—if, to take the
image further, one views golf as a game played with religious
fervor by Scots, who share it only reluctantly with others.
On this view, the movement from OT to NT is a fulfillment
in time but also a bringing together of those who were far
off with those who were near, the cross being the means by
which time's elective beginnings and adopting final purposes
are conjoined in Christ.

modern civilization as superior to that of the ancients and stopped looking to
them as models to imitate. The Fathers' deference to the past is perhaps the thing
about their writings which is most alien to the modern mind, and which creates
a barrier to our acceptance of them which is all the harder to surmount in that
it often goes unrecognized" (ibid.). Paul speaks in similar terms in Acts 17 about
the glories of bygone Athens.

Now this analogy fails as well, but it does illustrate something of the challenge of properly assessing the character of the OT and the achievement of a two-testament canonical witness, the second part of which uses the old, refers to the old, and allows the old a word of its own by the simple fact of its retention in a given form.[10]

And so here is what is at stake in the present work: the given character, material form, and influence of that first witness. One technical note at the start. I will refer to the tripartite form of the first witness as either the Hebrew text or the MT, even though the actual work of the Masoretes is a later development. I do this because in the lists that emerge, the Hebrew has retained this tripartite form without much alteration, even as we can spot minor divergences—for example, books in the Writings can move within the division; Josephus refers to a strange list, though it is unclear whether the question of his audience is pressing him for a special account; the talmudic tractate *Baba Batra* 14b has the order of the Major Prophets as Jeremiah, Ezekiel, Isaiah. The tripartite order is not preserved in printed Bibles in modernity, except in some Jewish publications, and in *BHS*.[11] The Law, the Prophets, and the Writings (Torah, Nebiim, and Ketubim—TaNaK) presents a challenging form, and we will be speaking of this form as an achievement.

This is especially true in the prophetic division. Twelve Minor Prophets existed from earliest times (so Ben Sira; Dead Sea Scrolls) as a one-book anthology in settled se-

---

10. See Childs's discussion in *Biblical Theology of the Old and New Testaments*, 70–79.

11. The Leningrad Codex has Chronicles in initial position, though *BHS* has moved it. See the careful and up-to-date analysis of Chronicles in recent theories on canon in A. E. Steinmann, *The Oracles of God* (St. Louis: Concordia Academic Press, 1999), 98–101. I am grateful to the PhD students at Concordia Seminary for pointing me to this book.

quence.[12] Isaiah, Jeremiah, and Ezekiel are combined with this to make up the "Latter Prophets." The historical-looking books of Joshua, Judges, Samuel, and Kings—the "Former Prophets"—comprise the first subdivision of this prophetic corpus. The Writings are not redistributed into new divisions but follow with their own integrity, variegated though it may be. Because English printed Bibles do not preserve this order, it is not as familiar to most readers.

Unfamiliarity, however, is not the only challenge when it comes to alternative lists. As an alternative term, "quadripartite" is not only a mouthful, and thus unwieldy; it is also not

---

12. In an excellent overview of the Twelve in the Dead Sea Scrolls, Watson (*Paul and the Hermeneutics of Faith*, 78–88) finds and shows conclusively that the traditional Twelve sequence is fully operational and without any rival. The Twelve exists in a wide variety of forms, and yet in all places where we can see the linkages between books and indications of sequence, the present MT sequence is attested. A Malachi-Jonah sequence had been proposed but then questioned severely. The evidence is simply too meager. There is no evidence of any single, so-called LXX order. This makes Barton's remarks questionable, including his general conception of a sole fixed structure in the Torah and all other books without order. At one point, he speaks of the order of the Twelve as one among many and considers it a convention of the Middle Ages. Speaking of Rendtorff's work on the canonical shape of the Twelve, Barton writes: "Even from a historical perspective, however, Rendtorff's discussion has something to contribute; for the 'canonical level' of the text is one that came into being at a particular time. That time, if we are to insist as he does on the order of the Minor Prophets in the present Hebrew canon, *is probably the Middle Ages*" (*Old Testament*, 286, emphasis mine). His general conception is stated in several works, but representative is this: "When NT writers refer to 'the law and the prophets' as a way of describing the Jewish Bible, 'the law' is fixed but 'the prophets' is still an open-ended list. All the books that are now in the Hebrew Bible were definitely included, but there was a penumbra of works which some approved, and which no one had yet proscribed" (*Making of the Christian Bible*, 77). Here the functional logic is clear, and the idea of a merely random collection of non-Torah writings is intimated. At another place he speaks of (what he considers to be) a later subdivision of the Writings from the Prophets based on chronology. So there is no intrinsic canonical ordering in the Twelve to be considered as crucial to the books' own integrity and tradition-history. Chronology is also a doubtful consideration in distinguishing Prophets from Writings (ibid., 42). On this, see below.

accurate, and it obscures the fact that the convention of modern printed Bibles—with law, history, poetic, and prophetic book divisions—has no true precursors. Several attempts have been made to describe the "theological achievement" of the fourfold, but one of them frankly acknowledges that this achievement would not have been grasped because in fact it is not preserved in antiquity in any of the major Greek recensions known to the church or synagogue.[13] In consequence, to speak of "the fourfold order" or the "Greek Bible" is to make too much of a single alternative sequence and one that did not actually exist until the arrival of modern printed Bibles.[14] It is hard to know, then, what to call these alternative listings. The appendix of a recent treatment of canon indicates the wide variety of sequences.[15] This fact must be assessed for its own significance.

One final note about the character of scholarship, especially in modern OT studies. More than thirty monograph treatments and a host of articles and collections of essays have been devoted to the study of the Minor Prophets. Interest in the coherence of the Twelve has surpassed that focused on interpreting the book of Isaiah as a sixty-six-chapter whole. The Society of Biblical Literature has recently hosted active and enthusiastic sessions on Isaiah and on the Twelve. I can refer to this exciting work only in piecemeal fashion, but it has gained wide acceptance as an appropriate model for interpreting the Minor Prophets both as individual books and as a collection. The debate is not so much about the "unity

13. M. Sweeney, see footnote 26, below.

14. C. Seitz, "Canon, Narrative, and the Old Testament's Literal Sense," *TynBul* 59 (2008): 27–34.

15. See the appendix of L. McDonald in McDonald and Sanders, *Canon Debate*: Malachi is never the last book. The Twelve often appear before Isaiah. The lists are quite varied. Daniel and Esther are often in final position.

of the Twelve" but about the character of that and the way the historicality of the individual witnesses is preserved or subsumed. The Twelve *is* a collection; the Twelve *are* individual books. An older approach that only recasts them in an alleged historical order and then reads them as individual works in an alleged historical context fails to grapple with the achievement of the whole in its present form. It ignores key interpretative indexes also deserving of the word "historical" as a statement of the way the prophets are meant to be heard as a whole.[16] Indeed, one recent commentator has had the temerity to refer to the older approach that seeks a single intention of Habakkuk directed to a single historical audience as "historically naïve and hermeneutically perverse."[17]

Yet there is a time lag between the unearthing of fresh discoveries concerning the Twelve and their incorporation into introductions to the Prophets, so these new findings are slow to take effect and become commonplace. Rolf Rendtorff's new theology of the OT, where the Twelve is treated as both an individual witness and a collection, is an exception that proves the rule.[18] The reasons for this lag time are neither conspiratorial nor high-flying but have to do with a wide variety of factors, which are documented in my recent monograph on the Prophets, *Prophecy and Hermeneutics*. My remarks here are dependent on that work.

16. See my essay on the species of history represented in the Twelve as a collection in C. Seitz, *Prophecy and Hermeneutics: Toward a New Introduction to the Prophets*, STI (Grand Rapids: Baker Academic, 2007), 216–18.

17. Watson, *Paul and the Hermeneutics of Faith*, 158.

18. Rolf Rendtorff, *The Canonical Hebrew Bible: A Theology of the Old Testament*, trans. David E. Orton (Leiderdorp: Deo, 2005). David Petersen has published a new introduction to the Prophets, and the order of the Twelve is the sequence followed, but there is no serious effort to treat the Twelve as a coherent collection.

Finally, I offer an explanation for this theme. Lee McDonald of Acadia Divinity College has written on the canon, and my former graduate student, Steve Chapman, published an impressive study called *The Law and the Prophets*,[19] which has recently been discussed by McDonald. Several years ago, I was privileged to think with and alongside Chapman in his work on canon. Two recent graduate students I have worked with have taken up the project of examining the third OT division, the Writings. I am aware that certain conservative scholars have sought to defend a closed and fixed Hebrew Bible, and this involves a combination of internal and external evidence.[20] But an impasse still exists. In my view, insufficient attention has been paid to internal editorial and canonical features that especially mark the formation of the prophetic division on the canon. Work on the Twelve has also not found its way into discussion of the canon, not to the degree needed.

It was also the untimely passing of my colleague at Yale and close friend, Brevard Childs, that pressed me to adopt for the Hayward Lectures a theme that touched on the canon. At the service of celebration and thanksgiving at Marquand Chapel, NT scholar, former dean, and close friend Lee Keck wrote these words:

> It is not surprising, therefore, that if there is one thing for which Childs is known, it is his emphasis on canon. More than anyone else, he insisted on exploring the theological consequences of the nature and history of the Christian two-testament canon. To make his case, he redefined the words "canon" and "canonization"; for him, "canon" refers to much

19. S. Chapman, *The Law and the Prophets: A Study in Old Testament Canon Formation*, FAT 27 (Tübingen: Mohr Siebeck, 2000).
20. R. Beckwith, *The Old Testament Canon of the New Testament Church* (Grand Rapids: Eerdmans, 1986).

more than the lists of books in the Bible; it really refers to the long process by which the Bible we have, and the texts it contains, came to be what they now are. And canonization is not something that was done to the writings; rather, some aspect of canonizing was occurring at every stage of the whole Bible-making process.

My concern in these chapters is to trace out the way the prophetic division of the Hebrew Bible was a canonical achievement of the first order. This achievement did not come at the closing phases but was there from the very beginning. The Law and the Prophets are the fundamental grammar of the scriptures of Israel, and the third division defers to that and works alongside it in its own special way. The NT also has its own character of deference, though it is of a highly specific nature given the subject matter with which it is dealing: the sending of the eternal Son in accordance with and in fulfillment of all that went before.

As a transition to the next chapter, consider the following two quotes and the larger conceptuality with which they work. The first is the "operating system" of John Barton in the context of canon and association.

> The "order" of the books in Scripture turns out, then, to be of small importance. Once an order is fixed and agreed on, all sorts of theological ideas can be read into it; but these are rationalizing explanations of something which in fact arose in large measure by accident than by design. In New Testament times there is very little evidence that "order" was an issue at all, except in the most obvious, chronological sense in which, for example, Joshua is "before" Judges. There is no clear evidence of lists before Josephus, and no list can have

had much effect on the way the Scriptures were understood before the use of codices became usual.[21]

In this conception, the existence of a "list" is what is needed to show that order was in effect.[22] Obviously, the Twelve at Qumran are "in order" and association, and the existence of a "list" to that effect is irrelevant. Second, canon is not about lists, and to prioritize this is to state the presupposition in advance. Barton makes it sound as if all efforts at association are secondary and contrived, and on that basis, "all sorts of theological ideas can be read into it." But order and association precede lists, and they are accomplishments of a deeply theological nature to begin with. This is obviously true of the Pentateuch (and its differentiation from the Deuteronomistic history), and it is true of the Minor Prophets as a collection.[23]

This view of the matter suggests itself to Barton because he has already moved to a position of what for him is the significance of an essentially bipartite division: a law collection and all other books in random or varied orders. This

21. Barton, *Spirit and the Letter*, 91.

22. In a recent work, Karel van der Toorn disputes the idea of lists from a different angle. He writes: "The Hellenistic period did not make a list but developed the notion of the era of revelation; the later list merely names the works believed to be genuinely from the canonical era" (*Scribal Culture and the Making of the Hebrew Bible* [Cambridge, MA: Harvard University Press, 2007], 249). He also speaks of a canon without closure as being crucial (ibid., 260). This is an important work that confirms many of the larger conceptual instincts of the present book. I was unable to consult it until these chapters were almost completed.

23. T. Collins also uses the complex final form of Isaiah to understand the Twelve as a collection (*The Mantle of Elijah* [Sheffield: JSOT Press, 1993]), and O. Steck has taken a similar tack in relating the final composition of Isaiah to the Twelve (*The Prophetic Books and Their Theological Witness* [St. Louis: Chalice, 2000]). This "critical" assessment is matched in lists of the books of the Bible, where the Twelve are never in final position but are always next to Isaiah, usually preceding it.

view flies in the face of the achievement of Law and Prophets in an ordered form.

Swete is far closer to the mark in his larger conceptuality when he attributes randomness and a penchant for "rationalizing" categorization to a movement into Greek dress that was not there at inception:

> When the law was translated into Greek, it was already a complete collection, hedged round with special sanctions, and in all forms of the Greek Bible it retains its precedence and has resisted any extensive intrusion of foreign matter. It is otherwise with the Prophets and Hagiographa. Neither of these groups escaped decomposition when it passed into the Greek Bible. The Former Prophets are usually separated from the Latter, the poetical books coming in between. The Hagiographa are entirely broken up, the non-poetical books being divided between the histories and the prophets. This distribution is clearly due to the characteristically Alexandrian desire to arrange the books according to their literary character or contents, or their supposed authorship. Histories were made to consort with histories, prophetic and poetical writings with others of their respective kinds. On this principle Daniel is in all Greek codices and catalogues one of the Greater Prophets, while Ruth attaches itself to Judges, and Canticles to Ecclesiastes.[24]

On this understanding, with which I generally agree, the order and association that exists in the grammar of Law and Prophets was a theological achievement. A secondary ordering, and others like it, occurs when this achievement is not sufficiently grasped, and often for very low-flying reasons adjustments are made. Swete sees this as a concern with literary genre, and that explanation is certainly possible.

---

24. H. B. Swete, *An Introduction to the Old Testament in Greek* (Cambridge: Cambridge University Press, 1900), 217–18.

But this fact will not be taken as grounds in these chapters for something like a concerted effort to eliminate all departures from the tripartite as deteriorations of form. The Writings are not in fixed form, and their migration is natural enough and often quite innocent. The danger, however, is twofold. One could choose to see great significance in a "rival order" when there is no such thing (either significance or a single rival order), or one could choose to see the existence of various orderings as a dismissal of the significance of association when that is manifestly not the case (either in the complex decisions that resulted in a Pentateuch ending with Deuteronomy rather than a Hexateuch or in the accomplishment we will highlight in the book of the Twelve). Isaiah is its own massive achievement of association.

It is this reality to which Childs pointed when he spoke of a "search for the Christian Bible."[25] He was not speaking of a "search for the Hebrew Bible" or a search for an adjudication of the various orders of the OT that exist in antiquity and in the Bible's reception history. He was honoring the status of the tripartite on something of the terms suggested above by Swete and over against either endless variety (with theology being "read in" and then "rationalized," so Barton) or a rival

25. Childs, *Biblical Theology of the Old and New Testaments*, 67: "One of the purposes of this attempt at a Biblical Theology is to apply these hermeneutical guidelines in working theologically within the narrow and the wider forms of the canon in search both for the truth and the catholicity of the biblical witness to the church and the world." Iain Provan is concerned with the implications of the language of "search" and of an apparent divergence from his prioritizing of the MT in OT introductions ("Canons to the Left of Him: Brevard Childs, His Critics, and the Future of Old Testament Theology," *SJT* 50 [1997]: 12–16). But Childs's language is chosen with care. He spoke of the MT as the lens for the canonical OT. The "search for the Christian Bible" indicates that the Christian church has in its long reception history handled the Bible in different canonical forms. This reality requires interpretation and careful assessment.

"Christian Bible" in Greek dress (Sweeney and others).[26] The Christian church "searches" for the Bible because the variety of listings that exist in its long life are the consequence of translation, custom, habit, innocent reordering, and the like. This fact should not be allowed to detract from the significance of the Law and the Prophets as the ground conceptuality of the OT as well as the stable form of the scriptures of Israel as these functioned to articulate the gospel of Jesus Christ in promise, prophecy, and figural anticipation.

26. Marvin Sweeney, "Sequence and Interpretation in the Book of the Twelve," in *Reading and Hearing the Book of the Twelve*, ed. J. Nogalski and M. Sweeney, SBLSymS 15 (Atlanta: SBL, 2000), 49–64; idem, *The Twelve Prophets*, 2 vols., Berith Olam (Collegeville, MN: Liturgical Press, 2000), 1:vx–xxix; idem, "The Book of the Twelve," chap. 5 in *The Prophetic Literature*, Interpreting Biblical Texts (Nashville: Abingdon, 2005), 169–209; idem, "Tanak versus Old Testament: Concerning the Foundation for a Jewish Theology of the Bible," in *Problems in Biblical Theology: Essays in Honor of Rolf Knierim*, ed. Henry T. C. Sun and Keith L. Eades (Grand Rapids: Eerdmans, 1997), 353–72. Sweeney is right to observe that a structure with the Prophets last, or as he has it, fourfold, "appears to have been set only after the widespread use of printed Bibles in the Western World" ("Tanak," 360). But then he reverts to a view that cannot be sustained: "It is based upon the order of books in the Vulgate, and prior to that, the order of various Greek traditions" (ibid.). This is simply not the case.

2

The Challenge of Order and Arrangement in Standard Old Testament Studies

If one follows the scholarly literature, it is clear that a cottage industry has grown up in recent years on the topic of canon. Among other things, this has meant fresh attention to the final form of the text and its relationship to genetic developments. Many of the studies focus on questions of authorial intention below/behind the received text and the wider legacy of historical-critical investigation into the Bible. These are literary, exegetical questions. For example, are there three Isaiahs and also an intelligible book of Isaiah? Is there Q and special Luke but also a Gospel form and a fourfold Gospel collection with John in meaningful position and Acts properly separated from Luke? One might also call this the theological or hermeneutical aspect of interest in canon.

But Anglo-Saxon scholarship has also shown great interest in historical and material canonical questions.[1] On this front, a serious impasse exists over the question of the stability of the OT at the time of the NT and whether it is possible to describe an OT canon constraining, informing, or otherwise declaring a proper theological horizon that was critical for the formation of NT convictions and, at ground, the mission of Jesus Christ. Was there an OT canon in the form of a closed collection of scriptural writings with authority? Or was the OT canon a consequence of only Jewish convictions or of only Christian convictions after decisions about the NT were already underway and even then going their own Christian way?[2] Does the church create the Bible (an old Roman Catholic/Protestant question), or does the Bible speak into the church and is received by it? The status of the OT (the scriptures of Israel; the oracles of God; "it is written"; "the Law and the Prophets") is crucial in this regard for the obvious reason that it exists in some form prior to Jesus Christ and the development of the NT canon, whose emergence we take to be dependent on the existence of a canonical conception rooted in the first witness.

In a recent version of this older debate, it is argued that a loose collection of various religious writings existed, some

---

1. See Brevard Childs's important distinction between Anglo-Saxon and Continental discussions of canon, in "The Canon in Recent Biblical Studies: Reflections on an Era," *ProEccl* 14 (2005): 26–45.

2. This position is held by Barr, Barton, Sundberg, McDonald, Allert, and others (for bibliography, see note 2 in chap. 1, above). J. Barton writes, "Obviously if one adopts Sundberg's definition of 'canon,' then canonization is a process of selection: 'canonization' is the name (*our* name) for the cumulative effect of decisions that various books should be excluded, the hardening up of rulings against the acceptance of *antilegomena*" (*The Spirit and the Letter: Studies in the Biblical Canon* [London: SPCK, 1997], 15).

of which found their way into a Christian Bible, and some of which did not; some of which influenced the way the NT took shape, and some of which did not.[3] Decisions about canonicity were then made on the basis of subsequent convictions and not due to pressure from a stable, authoritative, antecedent witness. On this view, perhaps one should say that by "OT canon" one means those writings of the OT that show up in the NT or in the early church in denser form than others (H. Hübner and Barton share similar views here, though from different angles).[4] That is, if reference to an OT canon means anything, it really refers to subsequent patterns of usage, revealing a grid of lesser and greater significance

3. A. Sundberg's phrase is "a wide religious literature without definite bounds" (*The Old Testament of the Early Christian Church* [Cambridge, MA: Harvard University Press, 1964]). Barton works with this understanding as well.

4. "Stuhlhofer [whom Barton cites with approval] has tried to establish some more useful categories by asking, statistically, about the intensity of citation and use of biblical books in the early Church" (Barton, *Spirit and the Letter*, 16). What actual use is made of this or that book becomes decisive. But surely the NT's use of the OT is determined by the subject matter with which it is concerned, which says nothing about the question of antecedent canonicity—unless one holds the theological/confessional view of Hübner that biblical theology involves only the OT *in novo receptum* and not *vetus testamentum per se*. However, for Hübner this is not an argument about canon but a particular confessional stance. Moreover, if the ante-Nicene fathers, for example, cite the OT books as often as they cite the NT, this could be an argument for a dialectical understanding of the canon of the early church, one at odds with the view of Hübner and Barton. Such "indexing" of citations from the early church fathers shows that the books of the Apocrypha are statistically marginal proportionally. And why, in an argument about the Son's begottenness, does a Greek father such as Athanasius appeal to Prov. 8 and not to Ecclesiasticus, and so forth? It is far from obvious that an appeal to subsequent use does anything but establish some interesting items in reception history, unrelated to canon strictly speaking. Even James Barr hints at the limitations of appeals to a conception of canon as citation (*Holy Scripture: Canon, Authority, Criticism* [Philadelphia: Westminster, 1983], 62n12). The statistical work is that of F. Stuhlhofer, *Der Gebrauch der Bibel von Jesus bis Euseb: Eine statistische Untersuchung zur Kanongeschichte* (Wuppertal: Brockhaus, 1988). See the alternative view of the early church fathers in E. Ellis, *The Old Testament in Early Christianity: Canon and Interpretation in the Light of Modern Research* (Grand Rapids: Baker Academic, 1991).

akin to what over time came to be called a "canon within a canon," which is of course no canon at all but an inversion of canonical comprehension in the name of selection and theological preference.[5]

If, on the other hand, one argues that the OT exercised pressure on the formation of NT convictions and that a stable authoritative canon existed at the time of the NT, several important challenges must still be faced. How many writings were in this canon? Does a canon need to be closed to be a canon? In what order were the writings arranged? Many have argued that the term "canon" means "stable, closed, in fixed order." Anything less should be called not "canon" but "Scripture" or "religious writings."[6] Here the obvious question is What is Scripture if it is less than canon but more than edifying literature, be it the Athenian Times, Homer or

5. The fixed meaning of the term "canon" as it applies to a NT canon or a single canonical Christian Bible is being used to constrain the variety of the witness, especially parts one may not like, by appealing to a particular principle of selection. For Martin Luther, it is "what commends Christ"; for Andrew Lincoln, it is "the pastoral needs of a community of faith." Lincoln's essay "Hebrews and Biblical Theology" appears in *Out of Egypt: Biblical Theology and Biblical Interpretation*, ed. Craig Bartholomew et al. (Milton Keynes, UK: Paternoster; Grand Rapids: Zondervan, 2004), 313–38, and is the subject of analysis in my forthcoming *Character of Christian Scripture*, STI (Grand Rapids: Baker Academic).

6. "The 'order' of the books in Scripture turns out, then, to be of small importance. Once an order is fixed and agreed on, all sorts of theological ideas can be read into it; but these are rationalizing explanations of something which in fact arose in large measure by accident than by design. In NT times there is very little evidence that 'order' was an issue at all, except in the most obvious, chronological sense in which, for example, Joshua is 'before' Judges. There is no clear evidence of lists before Josephus, and no list can have had much effect on the way the Scriptures were understood before the use of codices became usual" (Barton, *Spirit and the Letter*, 91). This judgment suggests itself to Barton because he has already moved to a position of what for him is the significance of a bipartite division: Law plus all others in random or varied orders. This ignores the achievement of Law and Prophets in an ordered form. H. B. Swete is more on target when he attributes randomness and categorization to a movement into Greek dress that was not there at inception (see note 24 in the previous chapter).

Dante, or even Aquinas or Calvin? And cannot a canon have authority independent of final closure? It is meaningful to speak of an "open canon."[7]

The present work will investigate these questions but will operate with one significant piece of information not usually incorporated into discussions of the canon. Recently, interest has been focused on the formation of two specific OT writings: the book of Isaiah and the book of the Twelve. In both cases, one is made conscious of the reality of affiliation and association within a diverse witness. These witnesses—the Minor Prophets and Isaiah—become something that decisions of closure or exclusion or delimitation could not achieve. They gradually seek internal relationship and association, and at a point in time, they cease from their labors and form a single, complex witness. This often happens in ways we can clearly see, as in the association of Hosea with Amos,[8] but in other places, the decisions are less evident, as in the placement of Joel, Obadiah, and Jonah. But the achievement of these twin works (Isaiah and the Twelve) is enormous, and once they reach a final stability of form, they resist further intrusion or adjustment. Because in each case the process of their coming to be took such a long time (and this is uncontroversial in the case of the twelve "Minor Prophets"), at the end of the process, they reflect a mature and hard-won canonical accomplishment, whose implications for the Prophets as a canonical division are wide-reaching and immediate.

7. See Iain Provan, "Canons to the Left of Him: Brevard Childs, His Critics, and the Future of Biblical Theology," *SJT* 50 (1997): 10–11.

8. See the fine work of J. Jeremias, "The Interrelationship between Amos and Hosea," in *Forming Prophetic Literature: Essays on Isaiah and the Twelve in Honor of John D. W. Watts*, ed. James W. Watts and Paul R. House, JSOTSup 235 (Sheffield: Sheffield Academic Press, 1996); and my fuller discussion in C. Seitz, *Prophecy and Hermeneutics: Toward a New Introduction to the Prophets*, STI (Grand Rapids: Baker Academic, 2007).

Failure to understand or to acknowledge this achievement has led to the notion that some parts of the OT canon have a fairly clear claim to order and stability (i.e., the Law)[9] while the remaining books are a diverse collection of individual religious writings only artificially organized or failing to take any shape at all until subsequent decisions ordered them into large-scale threefold, fourfold, or even more curiously arranged collections. Moreover, it is argued that these diverse and unorganized non-Mosaic books included more writings than those that ultimately found their way into the stable canon of Judaism.[10]

I hope then that the subtitle for the present study is becoming clearer. Early "canon formation" means that it is possible to conceive of canon and scriptural authority in phases prior to closure. The very fact that the canon of the Christian church entails a foundational expansion in the form of two testaments means that the respective scriptures of prophet (OT) and apostle (NT) have gathered to themselves an early canonical authority that involves association and stability alongside dynamic and eschatological elements. What is true of the development of a two-testament witness is true of the individual testaments as well. This dynamic in the first witness lies at the very heart of the Christian church's acknowledgment of a dual witness of two testaments—not a single tradition-history or a canon with greater and lesser parts or a two-stage canon where the first part dropped off entirely, like a booster rocket falling into the sea once it has

9. Strangely, Barton even tries to minimize this with reference to Swete's discussion of early church citations, where the "Law" is part of a wider collection of historical books (an octateuch). But Swete is very cautious here, and it is generally conceded, even by Barton, that the Law in both Christian and Jewish circles is an achievement—stable and foundational—of enormous proportion.

10. So Barr, Barton, McDonald, and others.

delivered its payload.[11] To speak of canon in these terms is to speak of Scripture's inner nerve: the word of God going forth to specific and ancient contexts but, because it is God's word, containing the seeds for later hearing, application, and fulfillment. To make closure determinative of canon ignores the dynamic that makes Scripture what it is from the beginning and throughout its process of becoming.

Reference to the "goodly fellowship of the Prophets" is intended to focus on the prophetic division of the canon as its own special achievement. If this achievement can be appreciated, the relationship of prophecy to law can be better clarified. Then it will be possible to talk about a foundational grammar, or conceptuality, that animates the scriptures of Israel and orients them around these two blocks of material.

This in turn will go a long way toward answering two questions that are fundamental to discussions of the material form of the canon of the OT. First, it helps explain what the remaining books of the OT are about, how they are different, and what the logic of them as "Writings" is. Second, it helps explain why final closing of the Writings, and therefore of the Hebrew Scriptures as such, is not as crucial to an account of canonicity and authority as has often been argued.[12] I judge these two points to be central to my argument in these chapters: (1) the Writings function in specific relationship to, and

11. On this achievement and alternative possibilities, see B. Childs, *Biblical Theology of the Old and New Testaments: Theological Reflection on the Christian Bible* (Minneapolis: Fortress, 1992), 73–79; C. Seitz, "Two Testaments and the Failure of One Tradition-History," chap. 2 in *Figured Out: Typology and Providence in Christian Scripture* (Louisville: Westminster John Knox, 2001), 35–47.

12. Indeed, it can amount to setting up a straw man to insist that canonicity has chiefly to do with closure, forcing one then to invent a new category different from it (i.e., "Scripture") whose actual character is then vague or only "not that." This was a significant part of the confusion created by Sundberg's appeal to a Scripture-versus-canon distinction.

with specific authority grounded in, the Law and Prophets, with the result that (2) the total number and final scope of this third division is not as decisive as is the achievement they represent in bringing out the importance of the Law and Prophets as the ground conceptuality of the scriptures of Israel, with which they work in conjunction. The final chapter will investigate in greater detail what the achievement of the Writings is and why it is a unique development, allowing the works to migrate in orders differing from the MT without thereby affecting their specific character as Writings.

In the course of this discussion, I will return to the more theological and hermeneutical implications of the material form of the canonical OT. But a practical matter lies close at hand. English printed Bibles typically separate Law and Prophets and introduce an order that departs from the tripartite form of the scriptures of Israel and is only loosely derived from a wide variety of actual Christian orders. I will not try to argue that the Hebrew order is somehow "purer" or insist that a tripartite structure become the newest publishing craze for English Bibles. Rather, the variety of orders and the divergence between a tripartite and a fourfold order (if that is what it is) needs simply to be understood.[13] There is a theological significance in the conjunction of Law and Prophets. That this is the source of modern confusion becomes obvious when a "prophetic ministry" is identified and valued primarily as something independent of foundations, law, creation, or a keen attachment to tradition and to continuity through time. The material, canonical separation of law and prophecy may be a practical reality that one can live with so long as theological significance is not read into what

13. Note the comments of H. B. Swete quoted in full near the end of the previous chapter.

is really an inconsequential decision to create new divisions of the books of the OT.[14] If the theological significance of the tripartite structure—what Childs called the lens only through which to understand the "canonical text"—is appreciated, then divergences from it can be accepted for what they are, and the major contribution of a Law, Prophets, and Writings achievement can remain untouched and theologically significant.

The Challenge of Order and Arrangement in the Canon

The discussion thus far has involved preliminary observations about the order of the OT canon and the theological implications of order. "The Law and the Prophets" is both a statement of order (something is first; the second thing is intimately related) as well as a productive theological construct—the Moses and Elijah of NT reference. We know the construct to be widely attested in virtually all Jewish sources of the period, and it is frequently retained in later Christian circles as well. It is also one standard and widespread way the NT refers to the scriptures of Israel.

Our examination is also carried out against a backdrop of general amnesia about why the matter of order ought even to be considered relevant, as indeed it was when the Bible was first being recast for introductory, historical, and theological reasons in the early nineteenth century. At that time, the matter was addressed with something like high moral urgency. This amnesia may make the argument difficult to follow since we have become accustomed to thinking of the

14. On the arrangement of G. von Rad's *Old Testament Theology* (trans. D. M. G. Stalker, 2 vols. [New York: Harper & Row, 1962–65]) and the implications of this, see my *Prophecy and Hermeneutics*, 61–73.

theological significance of order as something supplied by subsequent construal—whether that of the OT by the NT or through reception history in Jewish or Christian circles or via the popular modern interpreter offering a fresh and engaging way to view the subject matter. Does the OT itself have a commitment to order that is theologically important and necessary to observe? My answer to that question is yes, although the matter is complicated by the very diversity of the witness and its deep roots in a long history of development and ongoing theological transformation.

Of course, to speak of order is initially to foreshorten a basic canonical problem, the existence of differing orders. And here we touch on a matter of ongoing interest and considerable scholarly output: the relationship between basic structures like "the Law and the Prophets" and reconstructions of the OT and NT canon. It involves questions of consolidation and stabilization—closure and exclusion, as some have it—with respect to the canon. Although there were rival orders over against the tripartite structure of the MT, English printed Bibles have produced a now-conventional fourfold order (law, historical, poetic, and prophetic books, with Malachi immediately before Matthew) that cannot be traced to any single dominant ancient exemplar. This is in contrast to the single MT order now preserved alongside the various non-Hebrew listings. For example, the order of the Prophets in major Greek recensions—with Hosea, Amos, or Micah in signal position—is preserved nowhere in printed Bibles. Most Christian printing conventions follow a fourfold arrangement, with the Prophets last and preceding the NT. Fourfold orders do not exist in history; instead we have different listings that rarely have the same form and never have the Twelve in final position. If there is a modern printed text of a fourfold order, with the deuterocanonical books in the place they may appear in antiquity and the Twelve in the rare form of certain LXX recensions, it is not known to me.

Our concern at this initial point is in tracking the significance of order, any order, in standard studies of the OT. Brevard Childs offered a rival introductory model in his 1979 work, *Introduction to the Old Testament as Scripture*. In many ways, the groundbreaking character of that work had more to do with his treatment of individual books than with larger theological reflections on structure. On these larger matters, Childs was often cautious and (I know from personal conversations) concerned that his approach, with its focus on final form, might be taken to wrong extremes (e.g., structuralist readings, or approaches lacking clear historical roots and proper proportion).[15] Still, his work represented a shift by treating the books as individual works—as against the accidents of a tradition-historical process running out of steam—and by handling them in the order familiar from known Hebrew lists, that is, in a tripartite arrangement. That Childs did not give this arrangement sustained defense suggests that it operated at a more functional level. This bears further reflection.[16]

15. Structuralist and synchronic readings of biblical books held little interest for Childs because the historical dimension was usually dismissed or the diachronic was taken to be a challenge requiring harmonization.

16. I think Provan ("Canons to the Left of Him," 11–13) at this point overstates the difference between Childs's *Introduction to the Old Testament as Scripture* (Philadelphia: Fortress, 1979) and Childs's *Biblical Theology of the Old and New Testaments* (Minneapolis: Fortress, 1992). It is clear that Childs made an argument in favor of the order represented now in the MT and for its priority, and I have made a similar case. As stated below, the matter that remained latent, to my mind, was just how anyone wanting to adopt an arrangement that was canonical and not "historical" would have given attention to an order other than the tripartite. I also think that the tripartite order, especially in the area of "the Law and the Prophets," joins up better with the familiar accounts of historical criticism with which Childs and others are in discussion. Childs does not explicitly register this

At this juncture, it is important to clarify what is at stake in Childs's decision. So long as a sequential, genetic, historical account was a priority in standard OT works, the question of the order of the canonical writings was largely irrelevant. Authors simply dealt with matters of canon in an opening or concluding section. A "canonical order," in either Hebrew or Greek forms, is not straightforwardly historical. So it was that a decision to abandon it, made early in the nineteenth century, affected both forms equally. However, when one decides to think through the implications of canonical shaping and final form, then the question of order returns as a first-order affair. It even has implications for the structuring of a basic OT curriculum. A quick survey would probably indicate the significance of the exile or the efficiency of treating the historical books in one semester and the prophetic and Wisdom literature in the second, and yet neither semester lines up tidily with the canonical structures themselves.[17]

To illustrate, let us look at an example other than Childs. Rolf Rendtorff is committed to treating the OT books in

---

point, but the practical reality must be faced when one attempts to write an OT introduction with an internal arrangement based on the contents of the canon and not on a reconstruction below or behind them. In *Biblical Theology of the Old and New Testaments*, Childs was observing the fact of different arrangements of the Christian Bible as a totality in the church. In *Introduction*, he was speaking of the priority of the Hebrew in contrast to a different sequence of books in translational versions. In the latter instance, he was honoring the position of Augustine but was mindful that in practice Jerome had the argument that won out, in what in time would come to be called the Vulgate. In the end, Augustine adjusted his view of inspiration so as to speak of two inspired witnesses speaking to the church in the OT. Both Augustine and Jerome "searched," as it were, for the Christian Bible. My sense is that Provan believed Childs backed away from a commitment to the MT, when instead he was pointing to the peculiar reception history of a two-testament canonical witness in differing forms in the Christian church.

17. The category "Wisdom" makes the point nicely, just as Daniel resists easy classification in historical treatments.

their received form and has therefore decided on an arrangement, satisfactory to him, for his large-scale introduction and theology that correlates with the tripartite arrangement of the MT. His reasons for this are based on the place of Tanak in the Jewish tradition as well as on other considerations. In the course of his treatment, however, he notes the different fourfold arrangements found in English and German printed Bibles and attempts to give some account of them. The impression this gives, probably not wrongly, is that the fourfold order is derivative and represents a change from the received tripartite arrangement, whose essential character Rendtorff is at pains to evaluate. In his most recent work, moreover, and in essays he has produced on the Twelve, Rendtorff has joined a large group of scholars who insist that treatments of the Minor Prophets focus on the effect they produce as a single work and on the intentional character of that arrangement, through either painstaking reconstruction or a less ambitious accounting of editorial factors at work in their present organization. The implications of this for a standard introduction or theology of the OT are obvious and clearly stipulated in Rendtorff's most recent publication. The Latter Prophets are treated in the form we find them in the canonical Hebrew tradition and not in an alleged historical order or in an order known from other sources (e.g., LXX). Rendtorff's holistic reading of the Twelve is a dramatic departure from typical sequential accounts.

By contrast, Childs did not pursue the intention of the final form of the Minor Prophets in his *Introduction*, though his commitment to the canonical form meant that he treated them, not in some hypothetical historical sequence, but in the order presented in the MT. The transition from Hosea to Joel, a concern of Rendtorff and of recent literature, forms no part of his discussion (more on this below). One can also observe Childs's concern for Deuteronomy as an integral part of the Pentateuch, providing crucial hermeneutical guidelines for the appropriation of torah by later generations, and not as part of a Hexateuch or Deuteronomistic history (DtrH). It likewise follows that the canonical division of the Prophets makes absolute sense—both former and latter prophets—in the place we now find them. The critical index of the NT period and earlier—"the Law and the Prophets"—is then no curiosity but belongs to decisions deeply rooted in the history of the material. To transform this construct for the purpose of literary and historical speculation, in the manner of Sundberg and Barton, leads to the view that we have a fixed Torah and a sort of library of reading options, the bestsellers of which were under negotiation and later to be determined.[18]

For those who wish to provide comprehensive introductions to the OT based on a canonical order, it is relatively clear why the present tripartite order of the Hebrew would be chosen. The task and challenge is in relating this order to the historical-critical findings of the past two centuries, insofar as this is deemed appropriate and workable. One could choose a different order, say that of printed English Bibles, but it would require a substantial account of the historical and theological reasons for it, and these are not nearly so obvious as early critics of Childs conjectured them to be, despite the widespread popularity of the fourfold organization. Ironi-

18. Barton writes: "The Pentateuch was fully canonical—that is defended against addition or supplementation—by the first century BC, and all other Jewish books formed a fluid category, from which Jewish communities and writers selected *those they liked* or, perhaps, those they managed to get copies of" (*The Making of the Christian Bible* [London: Darton, Longman & Todd, 1997], 77, emphasis mine).

cally, the present tripartite order probably has more potential for linking it to historical-critical reconstructions than its fourfold counterpart, though Childs never raised this issue to the level of conscious reflection. This is particularly true of the relationship of law to prophecy in the history of OT traditions. Here the older discussion of Hexateuch and DtrH make clear the importance of Law and Prophets, especially when one allows the DtrH to remain operative in relationship to the Three and the Twelve—something the superscriptions of the Major and Minor Prophets underscore.

Another popular topic for reflection on canon, especially in English-language circles,[19] involves the status of the OT during the formation of the NT writings and the "canonical" status of them both. This discussion often emphasizes rival orders and the gradual closing of the canonical lists of OT books. A distinction is made between "Scripture" (having very loose authority and including books not now in the Hebrew tradition) and "canon" (a late and external decision to close a list and exclude certain books).[20] The wider collection of books is frequently compared to a Greek-language collection of Israel's scriptures (called "the Septuagint" for simplicity's sake), which we know at later times contained additional books and had a different organizational scheme.

Yet we really know very little about the origins of this Greek-language tradition and much less about its comprehen-

19. Childs ("Canon in Recent Biblical Studies" [see note 1 in the introduction, above]) points out that German-language work has been more interested in theological questions than in matters of scope and historical concern for closing. In the 2007 Vienna paper on canon (see note 15 in the introduction, above), G. Steins makes no mention of the views of Sundberg, Barton, Barr, and McDonald but instead engages the newer work of K. van der Toorn, A. de Pury, and S. Chapman.

20. See the insightful comments of Provan on the ambiguity of the appeal by Barr and Barton to "Scripture" as against "canon" ("Canons to the Left of Him," 10–12).

sive order and arrangement (the *Letter of Aristeas* speaks of a
Jewish translation into Greek of the Pentateuch only). In the
course of time, an order will appear in Latin that places the
Prophets in final position, assigns Lamentations and Daniel
to this category, and offers an alternative sequence for both
the Former Prophets and the Writings as these emerge and
are represented in the Masoretic tradition.[21] The greatest
challenge to holding an "open canon" position based on this
difference in order and the larger number of books included in
the LXX is the widespread use of the term "the Law and the
Prophets." It is difficult to see how this widespread use—it is
a fixed convention—could have persisted alongside a canonical arrangement so radically different (Law, historical books,
poetic books, prophetic books) and that retains no notion
of "the Law and the Prophets" as a bipartite reality. If one
wishes to argue that this bipartite order was essential in the
earliest form of rival orders too and was only subsequently
recast, then it is hard to see wherein the rivalry consisted save
in language, and the ground is cut out from under attempts
to differentiate between Greek and Hebrew canons. This is
Provan's point about Childs's ability to speak of canonical
authority and yet also of a potentially open (nonstatic) canon.
Closure does not authority make. It only confirms an authority and a stability well on their way to accomplishment.

To summarize, attempts to understand the order and arrangement of the canonical OT in relationship to the findings
of biblical criticism of the last two centuries bring to the
forefront questions of order and arrangement in the standard
accounts of OT introduction. This in turn raises the questions
of whether alternative orders ought also to be accounted for

---

21. On the complexity of the matter of orders in the early church fathers, see
Ellis, *Old Testament in Early Christianity*.

and where and how they emerged. On the one hand, scholars concerned with rival orders and with the slow closure of the OT canon after the development of a corollary set of NT writings wish to give priority to non-Hebrew canonical writings and orders. Yet it is the widespread appeal to "the Law and the Prophets" and the persistence of this conceptuality in the Hebrew order that complicates the argument for a distinction between Scripture and canon at the time of the NT's formation. The term "Law and Prophets" may have included books from the third section of what became the order of the Tanak, or it may have referred just to the two sections as we presently have them in that tradition, or both uses may have occurred. But this bipartite terminology is not so clearly seen in what will emerge as the large-scale traditions of the major Greek translations from the third and fourth centuries with their classical "Septuagintal form." They have not preserved a "Law and Prophets" conceptuality in a clear material form but have presented different kinds of orderings. Some of these may be close to the tripartite structure, but the Law-Prophets-Writings conceptuality is still disturbed to a greater or lesser extent, and new books (so-called deuterocanonical) are included in the lists. But even here we do not see a single rival form, much less the "fourfold order" we now find in printed English Bibles. In these recensions and in the early canon enumerations of the church fathers, the sequence of books is varied, and the logic behind the arrangement is unclear.

Our concern now is to show how the importance of order and arrangement emerges once we move beyond the reigning historical-critical depictions so prominent in introductions of the most recent period. Far from simplifying matters, however, this will require a fresh explanation of why the Hebrew order, as well as others, retains significance and a theological character.

The Form of an Introduction: A Brief History

Bernhard Anderson's famously successful *Understanding the Old Testament* offers an introduction that explicitly ignores the canonical presentation of the materials. The reason for this is taken as self-evident. Drawing on the general picture of biblical studies at the time, Anderson concludes that Israel's recital of faith is the key to "understanding the OT" and that—because such a recital (drawing on von Rad's notion of creedal affirmations in Israel) is, by nature, event-oriented— one should begin with the event that triggers all other event-reflections, the exodus. So that is how he structures the book at its beginning point, with lots of exciting rhetoric and examples from nonbiblical accounts of narratives concerned with historical memory. (No one has a memory of "creation" in the same event way).

It would have been rare for introductions of this period to have done otherwise, in whatever other ways they may have departed from Anderson's general approach. The order of presentation, assumed rather than argued, was the gift of the author in question and not of the material itself, or of the author tracking something said to be embedded in the literature below its present form. If one looks back to the nineteenth century, such an assumption was by no means self-evident.[22] But the point to be noted is that the historical recasting of the "theology of the OT" turned on a highly imaginative and creative set of assumptions about the basi-

---

22. See my recent account in part 1 of *Prophecy and Hermeneutics*.

cally orderless character of the Bible in its given form. I even have in my library a classic from the heyday of this period, which is titled *The Bible in Order*.[23] This of course makes the point nicely; why would the Bible "in order" not be the same as the Bible?

Common phrases from the period also give testimony to this state of affairs. Among them are the "Hexateuch (or Tetrateuch)," "Deuteronomistic history," "Wisdom literature," and "the Chronicler, Yahwist, Elohist, Priestly Writer." Also typical is an account of the Prophets that begins with Amos and ends with Jonah and that divides Isaiah in three; yet none of these terminological assumptions have any straightforward canonical correlate. Similar observations could be made about the NT.

Reflecting on the epochal nature of the work of von Rad, Rendtorff classifies his great teacher as a "semi-canonical" interpreter. He is referring to von Rad's order of presentation in his magisterial two-volume treatment of the canon of the OT, *Theology of the Old Testament*. By registering this observation, Rendtorff is subjecting von Rad's work to a criterion von Rad himself would probably not have recognized as relevant. The biblical material was there to be formed into the most compelling presentation, and von Rad would likely have said that the canon had very little to do with it.[24] However, Rendtorff's point is that von Rad moved from an account of the Hexateuch (itself a noncanonical entity) not to a discussion of the Prophets—thus matching the "Law and Prophets" assumption of the OT canon that

23. Edited by Joseph Rhymer (Garden City, NY: Doubleday, 1975).

24. Von Rad thinks that his order follows from an effort to lay bare how Israel thought about Yahweh. He writes, "The subject-matter which concerns the theologian is, of course, not the spiritual and religious world of Israel, . . . nor is it her world of faith. . . . Instead it is simply Israel's own explicit assertions about Yahweh" (*Old Testament Theology* [New York: Harper & Row, 1962], 1:105).

is also noteworthy in the NT—but rather to something he called (1) "the anointed of Yahweh" and (2) "Israel before Yahweh (Israel's Answer)." Volume 2 treated the Prophets and concluded with a section on OT and NT. "Israel's Answer," it should be noted, included not just Wisdom and Psalms but also treatments of the so-called Deuteronomistic and Chronistic histories.

What Rendtorff fails to note in sufficient detail is not just that von Rad's account was "semi-canonical" or, for that matter, noncanonical. Rather, in adopting this schema, von Rad actually reproduced something like a rival canonical presentation, that is, a fourfold order now evidenced in English (and German) printed Bibles. It would be too simple to call this order the "Septuagintal" order, though from some accounts of the history of the canon one might be forgiven for thinking that such an order was very relevant as the OT came to be (both in alleged order of books and an alleged larger number of books). But the problem is solved from another angle by all interpreters, von Rad included: all known orders are recast according to a historical sequence created from clues found in the biblical books themselves. So when one presses the matter to its conclusion, von Rad's order is only minimally "semi-canonical." The Prophets probably take it hardest at this point, in terms of both their canonical order and the intriguing juxtaposition of history (Former Prophets) and proclamation in the strange genre of books comprising the Latter Prophets. How can both types of literature be called "prophetic"? I think this is the problem that the rival orders attempt to resolve. This way of proceeding has persisted in OT introductions, histories, and theologies—especially in now-detachable accounts of the Prophets—and has only recently been questioned. So the position of von Rad and his brilliant contribution exist and persist within a wide and goodly fellowship.

Rendtorff also points to von Rad's efforts to link the Prophets with the Law via "pentateuchal traditions" as an example of his "semi-canonical" approach. But the claim is brought into question by von Rad's treatment and that of the preponderance of allied treatments when (1) the Law and Prophets are pulled apart and placed at the beginning and the end, respectively, in the presentation of the material and (2) the prophetic books are recast according to theories of origins, order, and development. This in turn has led to a view of the canon of the OT in NT times that makes the NT's use of the term "Law and Prophets" difficult to understand. The historical account of the "Law and Prophets" has been radically recast by OT scholars along very different evolutionary lines, making their conjunction the result more of external forces than of forces within the canonical process itself. In standard accounts of the period, "Law and Prophets" become phases in a developmental history that do not align very well with the presentation of introductions and theologies within which they function. This is obvious from the diachronic standpoint because of the late date of the Priestly writer, the early date of Amos, and the slowly evolving date of books like Psalms and Job (or Ruth and Ecclesiastes for other reasons).

Only with difficulty can von Rad's account be made to transition to a "Law and Prophets" model, because the Former Prophets have become a "Deuteronomistic history" and joined with a Chronistic one, and the historical sequencing of the Prophets themselves follows only after Wisdom has been expounded as part of "Israel's Answer." For von Rad, it is the Prophets that form the bridge leading into the NT, not something called "Writings."[25] As Chapman and others have shown, the process of canon formation is not anything so neat as one section closing after another. This point, at least, the standard introductions have made clear by their focus on the very complicated diachronic realities, however else they may have confused the canonical picture.

Famously or infamously, Brevard Childs presented a change in course by his 1979 *Introduction to the Old Testament as Scripture*. He was soon followed by Rendtorff himself, as well as by accounts of the presentation of the canon unexamined in his own 1979 treatment. This is particularly true of the Minor Prophets but also of the Writings. Changes in the interpretation of Isaiah also slowly took place through the works of Peter Ackroyd and Ron Clements.[26] Rendtorff had gone a long way in questioning the happy alliance between form-critical and documentary accounts of the Pentateuch in his 1977 analysis, and Blenkinsopp, Sheppard, and others had already been working steadily on the complex canon-formation issues that led to a "separation" or recasting of Hexateuchal and Deuteronomistic histories into the present Pentateuch and Former Prophets.[27]

I want to call attention primarily to developments in the prophetic division of the canon. As we have seen, Childs reinstated interest in the tripartite order, for both historical

25. R. Rendtorff attempts to handle the von Rad presentation and the present canonical tripartite form with sympathy in his brief remarks in *The Canonical Hebrew Bible: A Theology of the Old Testament* (Leiden: Deo, 2005), 1–12.

26. P. Ackroyd, "An Interpretation of the Babylonian Exile: A Study of 2 Kings 20, Isaiah 38–39," *SJT* 27 (1974): 329–52; R. Clements, "Beyond Tradition-History: Deutero-Isaianic Development of First Isaiah's Themes," *JSOT* 31 (1985): 95–113.

27. R. Rendtorff, *Das überlieferungsgeschichtliche Problem des Pentateuch*, BZAW 147 (Berlin: de Gruyter, 1997); J. Blenkinsopp, *Prophecy and Canon* (Notre Dame, IN: University of Notre Dame Press, 1977); G. Sheppard, *Wisdom as a Hermeneutical Construct*, BZAW 151 (Berlin: de Gruyter, 1980).

and practical reasons, as a way to structure OT introduction. The book of Deuteronomy—by intimating an order of prophets to follow and insisting that future generations under that new order find themselves always with the fathers at Sinai—created a radical closing of one canonical section and a maximal relating of two evolving canonical sections.

But this second section was itself a combination of materials of varied and diverse contents and origin. The most obvious challenge to conjunction was the merging of a former and a latter prophetic witness, the first consisting of continuous narrative, for the most part, and the second more obviously bearing the classification of prophetic: the Three Major and Twelve Minor Prophets. That this conjunction was an achievement of no small proportion is indirectly reflected by its recasting, or otherwise alternative emergence, as historical and prophetical divisions of an alternative order, themselves further divided by a fourth category called poetic, wisdom, or lyrical books. Childs and others have gone a long way in explaining how Deuteronomy was released from the duty of introducing a continuous history running to the end of 2 Kings (called Deuteronomistic) to become instead the final and pivotal conclusion of the foundational "torah" section.[28] But what of a decision to unite this erstwhile Deuteronomistic history with an evolving prophetic corpus and eventually to find patterns of consolidation within this second division that would have implications for the remaining books of the canon?

---

28. Childs, *Introduction*, 232–38; J. Sanders, *Torah and Canon* (Philadelphia: Fortress, 1972); J. Blenkinsopp, *Prophecy and Canon* (Notre Dame, IN: University of Notre Dame Press, 1977); S. Chapman, *The Law and the Prophets: A Study in Old Testament Canon Formation*, FAT 27 (Tübingen: Mohr Siebeck, 2000).

Here Childs offered only provisional clues, a matter I will seek to rectify in the following chapter. His chief focus was on reinstating, in the light of two centuries of hard historical-critical work, the logic of individual witnesses, especially that section of the Prophets that had come to be termed "Latter." He paid particular attention to the unity of Isaiah and to signs of the redactional concern for hearing its sixty-six chapters as an orchestral achievement rather than as a series of solo performances. Frequently, space limitations permitted Childs nothing more than a rehearsal of dominant trends in research and a chance to offer clues about where the work needed to move forward in order to account for the logic of the final form.

It is clear that subsequent readers, and later Childs himself, threw themselves especially into work on the book of Isaiah, so that commentaries no longer focused on defending a straightforward eighth-century authorship of Isaiah but reflected the consensus in critical literature that one needed to account for the whole book and not just for three alleged Isaiah authors and books.[29] Jeremiah has proved a less-fruitful area of research, though time may alter this. Qumran reveals that the book had several competing orders and different scope; flexibility and careful argument will be required to meet this challenge.

Childs's introduction frequently offers great insights on the Minor Prophets, but he generally focuses on understanding how the analysis of historical criticism failed to see the hermeneutical significance in the development of later levels of tradition. This allowed him to assess historical criticism

---

29. B. Childs, *Isaiah: A Commentary*, OTL (Louisville: Westminster John Knox, 2001). My two commentaries on Isaiah, one in the Interpretation series and the other in the New Interpreter's Bible, also work this ground.

critically and to make judgments about what was and was not a fruitful critical insight. So, for example, he could accept much of Hosea scholarship's understanding of subsequent levels of redaction, but he did not believe their appearance required a reconstruction that lifted their significance into the realm of history rather than into the service of a final literary and theological achievement now represented in the final form of Hosea (more on this in the next chapter). There was indeed a "Judah redaction," but Childs wanted to understand its hermeneutical function in the shape and movement of the book of Hosea rather than the trail it led into the history of religion or history of traditions. Similarly, he asked why there were psalms in Habakkuk and Jonah and what their appearance achieved hermeneutically? Micah and Isaiah traditions appear to have influenced each other, especially in the complex final form of Micah. How should this affect our reading of them, both individually and in light of each other? Amos contains what some consider a mitigating gloss. For Childs, this conclusion did not get at the question of how the book could undergo subsequent editing and still retain its larger hermeneutical effect as the harsh message of an eighth-century, flesh-and-blood prophet, a message mitigated only through the lens of judgment rooted in God's own character.

The explanation for these readings, of course, could be found in the way Childs creatively worked with the findings of historical criticism, within the confines of an individual book and the research that had also worked largely individually with them as single prophetic persons. This individualization of the witnesses came from the nineteenth-century decision to relocate the prophets on a grid of historical sequencing, beginning with Amos and ending with Joel, Jonah, or Malachi. The salutary instinct here was the desire to give us flesh-and-blood men and women of God, forthtellers to real generations in a real space and time. Even the efforts of von Rad and others to find their association in traditions they held in common essentially left untouched the depiction of them—salutary though it may have been—as individuals. Von Rad would have found it strange indeed to think that Amos and Hosea ought to share anything, unless it could be shown at the level of their actual knowledge of each other in history or in reconstructing the traditions they shared—which in both cases amounted to nothing.[30]

Childs began to see associations at a different level: in the way the historical prophet was related by editors to future generations so that these generations might with all seriousness appropriate a message from the past. The original message was not confined there because it was intentionally shaped to speak to future readers as well as to historical audiences, as in Amos's "two years before the earthquake." In the case of Micah, for example, this might indicate fields of association laterally established in the canon, as with Isaiah and his picture of the restoration of Zion; or with Joel and prior prophecy; or with Habakkuk and the Psalter; or with Malachi and the editing of the prophetic corpus as a whole; or with Hosea and the proper stance of wisdom necessary to grasp God's ways.

In the meantime, a new picture has opened up, one unforeseen in the published pages of Childs's *Introduction to the Old Testament as Scripture* but kindred to concerns he had expressed about the single witness of Isaiah being divided not into twelve but into three, with its many editors and editions totaling nearly a dozen. The Minor Prophets

---

30. Seitz, *Prophecy and Hermeneutics*, 155–87.

have a high degree of literary cross-reference (call it a form of association), but an approach that seeks to individualize the witnesses can understand this connective tissue only on the theory of peripheral final editing. For all intents and purposes, this cross-referring among the Twelve ceased to hold any interest for scholars, and in Childs it also plays little if any role. The Prophets were rearranged according to theories of when they spoke and how an ordered presentation might take advantage of this. Introductions to the Prophets saw this as their bread and butter, and over time the historical and introductory sequence of the "classical prophets" (a term invented when the canon ceased being a proper lens) became relatively fixed (as with the Letters of Paul).

I will not try to explain why this aspect never emerged with clarity in Childs's 1979 *Introduction*. Perhaps just getting us to deal with the carefully edited form of the individual witnesses as we have them was a sufficient challenge for him. But one factor was there for possible development, and it connects with our attempt to understand the logic and theological character of "the Law and the Prophets" as a strongly associated witness. By treating the Prophets in the order of the MT, it is possible to tease out the implications of the following:

1. Resistance to changes in the order of the Twelve even in printed Bibles organized according to a fourfold arrangement;
2. Consolidation of this Minor Prophet collection with the Three, and the curious case of Daniel; and especially
3. Creation of a prophetic division that brings into one section the narrative books of Joshua, Judges, Samuel, and Kings and the Major and Minor Prophets.

If we can better understand this consolidation, we may also begin to see the logic of the disparate third division and why the logic was constantly disturbed or recast in alternative orders until well into the Christian era.[31]

31. Perhaps this was tied up with the use of Latin and its persistence in Catholic Christendom, thus leading to a relatively stable order in the Middle Ages, the exemplar for modern printed Bibles. See note 5 in the next chapter, below.

3

The Achievement of Association in the Prophetic Canon

My focus in this chapter is on the associative moves that created a prophetic division of the canon, thus bringing together a book of the Twelve, three Major Prophets, and the four narrative books of Joshua, Judges, 1–2 Samuel, and 1–2 Kings, and now comprising Former and Latter Prophets in one single division. Subsequent to this, in some lists we find other books—such as Chronicles, Ruth, or Lamentations—intruding into the second division, but these are minor exceptions. Their intrusion may indicate that the line between Prophets and Law was firmer than that between Prophets and other books, but it does not indicate that the crucial "Law and Prophets" conceptuality was ever in doubt at the period when the canon was consolidating. Historical-critical and canonical methods agree on the accomplishments indicated within the prophetic division: the Deuteronomistic history (Joshua, Judges, Samuel, and Kings), the final form of Isaiah, and the book of the Twelve. In the later postbiblical period, it would take time before the large-scale recensions of the so-called Septuagint would indicate a new set of classifications, with Prophets sometimes separated from Law and ranged alongside new categories of Historical and Poetic books. As noted above, even this is too tidy a description.[1] Our present task is to understand the unique formation of the prophetic division. Critical in this regard is the book of the Twelve.

At the conclusion of this chapter, I will suggest what role I believe the third canonical division plays, why it is different, why its internal association is of a different order, and why its closure is less decisive than has been maintained, especially by those who have judged closure to be a major factor in the assessment of canon. A proper appreciation of the Writings, as opposed to the Prophets or the Law and Prophets, also strikes at the heart of the claim that what we had at the time of the NT was a stable Mosaic corpus followed by a loose collection of writings capable of being referred to as prophetic and so constituting the second division of writings referred to in the NT by the term "the Law and the Prophets." My

1. Codex Vaticanus places the Twelve before Isaiah, Jeremiah, and Ezekiel and concludes with Daniel. Codex Sinaiticus concludes with five of the Writings (Psalms, Proverbs, Ecclesiastes, Song of Songs, Job). Codex Alexandrinus resembles Sinaiticus (which is missing books), and it too retains a form not far from being tripartite, with "Former" Prophets (including Ruth and Chronicles) followed by the Twelve and the Three ("Latter" Prophets). The same Writings are at the close, joined with a greater number of allied deuterocanonical works (e.g., Tobit, Judith, Wisdom, et al.). Great care must be taken not to read the convention of modern printed Bibles back into the early reception history, even of the so-called LXX. Earlier lists from church fathers do not show a consistent order, which suggests that there was not a strong "rival" tradition in Greek or Latin dress but simply a variety of ways to enumerate the books. The major uncial traditions of the LXX are not themselves uniform and can be seen as both similar to and different from the tripartite form.

arguments thus far have strongly questioned this position. Let me summarize the key points:

1. Those arguing for a late closing of the canon and for a sharp distinction between a loosely defined, varied set of scriptural writings and the authoritative "canonical works" must emphasize the existence of rival orders and enumerations. Yet the persistence of a "Law and Prophets" conceptuality is hard to deny, nor can one find a rival articulation in the NT period. Whatever else may be said about the totality of the Writings and their limits, it is possible to speak of an "open canon" and not to equate closure with canonicity or authority. Rather, in this early association of Law and Prophets and its widespread conventionality, we see a trend toward stabilization in evolving witnesses and in the authority of a growing scriptural witness. A clear authorizing process is at work within the bipartite association itself, with the Prophets emerging as successors to Moses and the ensuing generations constrained by the foundational Sinai covenant made with him, his generation, and those about to enter the promised land. A sharp distinction between canon and Scripture has confused this issue and has blurred the accomplishment of the canonical process in stages prior to closure or stabilization. This is as true for the canonical development of the NT (where a fourfold Gospel collection is analogous to the Pentateuch) as it is for the OT.[2]

2. If one moves away from historical grids for OT introduction toward a canonical grid, it is difficult to make

2. See my discussion in *The Character of Christian Scripture*, STI (Grand Rapids: Baker Academic, forthcoming).

a case for the fourfold arrangement found in printed
Bibles since it is not actually found in any single form
in antiquity. Childs's decision to pursue a tripartite
introduction is therefore historical, theological, and
practical. It is hard to imagine an introduction that
could use a "fourfold form" with equally widespread
and balanced support. When Childs speaks of a "search
for the Christian Bible," he is not gainsaying this insight but is simply pointing, as did Karl Barth, to the
empirical reality that Christian churches do not have
one form of Christian Scripture. This is not to say that
certain foundational assumptions—theological, historical, and practical—are beyond our grasp.[3] Nor would
it be preferable to grant authority to decisions that
occur in the life of the church for other reasons (such
as translational language, custom, or church practice),
making the authority of Scripture posterior to churchly
authority. Here the specific, antecedent role of the OT
must be appreciated.

3. Childs's adoption of a tripartite form for his *Introduction* led to an ironic discovery: if one wants to build on
historical-critical findings and move beyond them for
the purpose of a canonical introduction, the fourfold
order is not very useful. Where it does appear, as in
ghostlike form in the superstructure of von Rad's OT
theology, it is largely accidental and unprocessed, and I
suspect that it appears for other than historical-critical

3. Provan is concerned about a shift in position by Childs, but the precise
wording is important. Childs does not speak of a "search for the tripartite Old
Testament," because it is a stable reality. The final form is there to be evaluated,
including its diachronic depth. The "search for the Christian Bible" entails a biblical theological and exegetical task regarding the proper handling of the Old and
New Testaments, given the material form of the whole Bible as this exists within
the history of the Bible's reception in the church.

reasons (e.g., wanting the Prophets to build a bridge to the NT, a point I pursue with some vigor in *Prophecy and Hermeneutics*). The appearance of a fourfold structure in von Rad is not comprehensively executed or consciously argued for, and the transition from a Hexateuch to "The Anointed of David" happens at a level arguably different from whatever is going on in the later orders of the LXX and kindred listings. His chief interest appears to be in placing the Prophets in final position so as to assist his understanding of tradition-historical and typological movement from OT to NT.

Why an order different from Torah-Prophets-Writings emerged or why in (what will become) Septuagintal texts one can spot a strange order for the Minor Prophets or within the book of Jeremiah are intriguing questions. Some see the emergence as a Christian development intended to have the Prophets come last and so "lean into" the subsequent witness of the NT, and this view has even been stretched to include the peculiar ordering of the first three books of the Twelve.[4] Support for this view is by no means clear, however; the existence in the early church of Greek-language OT Scriptures with orders close to the present tripartite arrangement show the explanation to be too simplistic.[5]

In this chapter, I will survey recent work on the Twelve and anticipations of these hermeneutical insights in Childs's

4. M. Sweeney (see note 26 of chap. 1, above).

5. One must also be careful to distinguish the work of Jerome as translator (which itself went through phases) both of individual books and of groups of books from an "order" said to be that of "the Vulgate." Jerome's own statements and reconstructions of his scholarly procedure suggest that the tripartite is the order he most gravitates toward. It may possibly be the work of Cassiodorus (mid to late sixth century) that resulted in an order that stamped the Latin Bible and led to the conventions more familiar in the modern period. But this is speculation.

own work, especially in Hosea. But I also wish to understand
the implications of the consolidation of a Minor Prophets
corpus—a unified and structured book of the Twelve—for
the emergence of the canonical division of Prophets, which
came in time to include the narrative books of Joshua through
Kings and the three Major Prophets as well. The stabilization
of this form is a unique achievement. It may also say something about the division of the third section, the Writings,
if not its emergence in the first instance. Armed with these
insights, we can then address an order that has gone its own
way, with the Prophets in final position and a fourfold rather
than a (bipartite en route to) tripartite structure.

The Minor Prophets

The sections in Childs dedicated to reflection on the second division of the canon and its internal classifications—"former"
and "latter" prophets—are very brief.[6] In the case of the
Minor Prophets, or "book of the Twelve," Childs registers
awareness of early attention to this collection as a unity in
Ben Sira and also to scattered clues for some principles of arrangement in the development of the literature (catchwords,
as in the end of Joel and the beginning of Amos), but that is
all. As stated already, Childs's chief concern is with the individual witness and the logic of the witnesses as works with
their own integrity as finished products. Special attention is
given to the hermeneutical effect of later additions.

Even at the time of the writing of Childs's introduction,
scholars were beginning to consider the editorial arrangement
of the Twelve. The protégé of von Rad, Hans Walter Wolff,

---

6. Brevard S. Childs, *Introduction to the Old Testament as Scripture* (Philadelphia: Fortress, 1979), 230–38, 306–10.

was hard at work on the Minor Prophets for the Biblischer Kommentar series. In his commentary on Joel and Amos, Wolf wrote:

> In all likelihood those who arranged the collection of the Twelve wished us to read Amos and the following prophets in the light of Joel's proclamation. For manifest in Joel is a comprehensive view of prophecy closely akin to that governing the prophetic corpus in its final, canonizing intention.[7]

In the NICOT series, Leslie Allen noted that Obadiah "may have been viewed as a virtual commentary on Amos 9:12."[8]

A survey of older commentaries on the Twelve (Pusey and previously) also shows an interest in the literary connections that surface when one reads the Twelve closely, one book following the next, rather than in trying to assign them new historical locations and then attributing these associations—if any longer of interest—to secondary editing, subsequent arrangement, juxtaposition, and the like. Rather, the prophets knew one another and could use each others' words for effect. Pusey is the last critical commentator to preserve this naive view, backed up with scientific energy and now defended on the terms of modern historical inquiry.[9] John Calvin once argued that Amos (1:2; 9:13) used Joel's public speech ("The LORD roars from Zion" and "mountains shall drip sweet wine" [3:16, 18]) so as to underscore his prophetic authority. This was necessary for a man who admitted, "I am no prophet,

7. Hans Walter Wolff, *Joel and Amos: A Commentary on the Books of the Prophets Joel and Amos*, Hermeneia (Philadelphia: Fortress, 1977), 4.

8. Leslie C. Allen, *The Books of Joel, Obadiah, Jonah, and Micah*, NICOT (Grand Rapids: Eerdmans, 1976), 129.

9. E. B. Pusey, *The Minor Prophets with a Commentary*, 2 vols. (Oxford: Parker, 1860).

nor a prophet's son" (7:14), although Calvin saw in him the unmistakable profile of a spokesman for God. Examples like this could be compounded because the literary cross-references are so obvious when one reads these books serially.

Childs was aware of Wolff's notion of redactional levels in Hosea, and he agreed that there was evidence of subsequent levels of tradition throughout the book. However, he objected to the overly speculative account of this in Wolff (the history-of-religions reconstruction) and to attempts at finding more levels than was warranted for understanding the book as it now stands, such as assigning to these levels specific intentions and specific historical occasions in the development of the tradition. Childs saw in Hosea a realistic critique of false worship and corrupt understandings of fertility, a critique expressed both by the prophet's message and by God's use of Hosea—through his marriage to Gomer—as a sign-act for the northern kingdom. In this sharply realistic and highly specified attack on cultic abuses lay the potential to say something about God's people more generally. So the language was extended metaphorically to the realm of spiritual infidelity and to their failure to remember God and his provision ("lack of knowledge"). The potential was there in the historical preaching of Hosea.[10]

A Judah redaction related Hosea's message to the southern kingdom, contrasting Judah's ultimate fate in a hopeful way, but also warning Judah not to do as Israel had done. (One can find a similar pattern of comparison in the opening chapters of Jeremiah, which is again turned to ironic effect against Judah.) A final redaction of the book of Hosea provided the concluding verses: the wise were those who saw not only what the prophetic word said in its own day but also what

10. Childs, *Introduction*, 373–84.

it, under God, continued to say as it reached out to include them and their generation. Like the Judah redaction, which protected the southern kingdom from historicizing God's word to Israel, the wisdom redaction sought to teach future generations how to read the completed book of Hosea as a word from God enclosing and anticipating generations that God alone had in view. The wise were taught by God's word. In this, they showed understanding of God's ways—that is, his character and his providential overseeing of time—and how to walk in them.[11]

Writing after Childs's 1979 introduction and working largely independently of this discussion, a student of Wolff, Jörg Jeremias, accepted the depth dimension of Hosea set out by Wolff, but he turned it in a fresh direction. In Jeremias's view, these editors were in fact pupils of Hosea, and they edited Hosea with the help of Amos, and Amos with the help of Hosea.[12] Future generations were learning to read not just Hosea but also other prophetic books in light of one another. Lessons of social misconduct and cultic abuse were two sides of one coin, which the mutual editing of the books sought to make clear. Jeremias does not deny the singular and the individual, so highly prized by historical work, but believes that those who shaped the material wanted the readers to understand the relationship of Amos to Hosea and vice versa. This, after all, has its own character of historical reflection. Here also is the explanation for why Hosea, arguably the

11. I am indebted to the brilliant treatment of Raymond Van Leeuwen for an elaboration, undertaken independently, of Childs's view. See R. C. Van Leeuwen, "Scribal Wisdom and Theodicy in the Book of the Twelve," in *In Search of Wisdom: Essays in Memory of John G. Gammie*, ed. Leo G. Perdue, Bernard B. Scott, and W. J. Wiseman (Louisville: Westminster John Knox, 1993).

12. J. Jeremias, "The Interrelationship between Amos and Hosea," in *Forming Prophetic Literature*, ed. J. W. Watts and P. House, JSOTSup 235 (Sheffield: Sheffield Academic Press, 1996), 171–86.

younger prophet according to standard historical treatments, nevertheless precedes Amos. According to Jeremias, the pupils of the prophet Hosea were more influential after the fall of the northern kingdom confirmed Hosea's prophecies, and they thus had more influence in editing Amos than Amos did over Hosea. By placing Hosea first canonically, the message of Amos would be heard through the lens of Hosea, especially with respect to God's character. The explanation for what have been called "mitigating glosses" in Amos also lies close at hand: they are not prophecies "after the fact" or "happy endings," but God's one word vouchsafed to Hosea, enlarging and clarifying Amos's denunciations of Israel.[13] Israel would fall, but God's final word would be cleansing and purging and restoration. This is what the wise are taught when they understand God's ways.

A further aspect of this approach, unforeseen by Childs, has to do with the placement of Joel, which immediately follows Hosea. Hosea ends with a call to repentance and an exhortation to the wise. Joel portrays a generation responding to Hosea's appeal, beseeching God in repentance and contrition and appealing to God's character as revealed in Hosea, a character in relationship to which Hosea's children ("Not my people"; "Not pitied") are named and renamed, the compassionate LORD attached to a people. The "Who knows?" anticipation of the king of Nineveh, uttered by Joel's audience, is answered by God's acts of mercy and his restoration of bounty and fertility, which had been withdrawn

13. The careful handling of this issue by G. A. Smith is theologically astute. The problem, however, is created by the sequential-chronological model Smith has inherited. "The Problem Amos Left," as he puts it, is a problem because Hosea has been read after Amos and in a way highlighting the individuality of the prophets. See my discussion in C. Seitz, *Prophecy and Hermeneutics: Toward a New Introduction to the Prophets*, STI (Grand Rapids: Baker Academic, 2007), 130–34.

in Hosea's day and again more severely in the days of Joel ("Has such a thing happened in your days?" [1:2], referring to the locust assault).[14] Then this singular act of repentance and restoration in the days of Joel is made a type for God's work with the nations and with creation itself in a great and terrible day of the LORD. God in creation, in deliverance in Egypt, in episodes of judgment and mercy with his people, and with the nations on account of them—all of these acts fill in the content of what it means to speak of the day of the Lord. This is why Wolff can say that Joel offers a comprehensive vision, enabling us to understand the prophets that follow, especially Amos and Obadiah.

Further discussion of research on the book of the Twelve is not necessary to support the basic point being made. What Childs saw in Hosea as an effort of association via editorial expansions aimed at future generations, subsequent scholarship on the Twelve has identified within, across, and

14. James D. Nogalski reads Joel so tightly with the preceding Hosea that he takes the referent to mean: Has such an act of repentance, such as was called for by Hosea's final chapter, happened? The answer then, according to Nogalski, is No. It is this kind of blending of the books that has brought strong criticism from E. Ben Zvi. In *Prophecy and Hermeneutics*, I have endeavored to keep a proper balance between the individuality of the witness and the total effect of the Twelve, and here the diachronic aspects are critical. Nogalski's work appears in *Literary Precursors to the Book of the Twelve*, BZAW 217 (Berlin: de Gruyter, 1993); and idem, *Redactional Processes in the Book of the Twelve*, BZAW 218 (Berlin: de Gruyter, 1993). E. Ben Zvi has a representative essay in "Twelve Prophetic Books or 'The Twelve': A Few Preliminary Considerations," in *Forming Prophetic Literature*, 125–56. The integrity of the individual witnesses is something Childs stressed, and attention to the Twelve as a whole must honor that. Making any single book the hermeneutical key to the whole also threatens this fundamental canonical insight. Joel serves this purpose for some (e.g., Nogalski, to a degree; Rendtorff; Wolff), and Habakkuk for others (e.g., F. Watson in *Paul and the Hermeneutics of Faith* [Edinburgh: T&T Clark, 2004]). Joel's referent in the opening question of 1:2 is to be found within the book of Joel, that is, it is the locust plague, a plague without precedent: "Have we ever seen a plague like this before?" But the act of repentance, which does take place within the book of Joel (2:12ff.), is an act in positive response to the horizon established by the book of Hosea in its canonical form.

comprehensively throughout the Twelve as a whole. This is accomplished not in one single way but variously, due to the historical reality of there being individual prophets speaking at individual moments. The way of their association is therefore as specific and individual as the original witnesses themselves. If Jeremias is right about the starting point of Amos and Hosea, it is unlikely that any prophet or prophetic book stood alone for any length of time, and some may have been generated specifically in relation to a growing corpus so as always to belong to a goodly company of prophets.[15] The case must be examined book by book, but the growing consensus is of twelve witnesses of integrity, outfitted to speak both as twelve and as one.

The same point has been made in the case of Habakkuk and other books. Jonah's denouement, many argue, is found later in the book of the Twelve.[16] Zephaniah's placement is more thematic than historical (Habakkuk most likely prophesied before Zephaniah), and this allows Zephaniah—with its very full "day of the LORD" emphasis—to accomplish the transition to Haggai. One historical aspect of the "day of the LORD" is surely the destruction of Jerusalem in 587, presupposed by Haggai and a central concern of Zephaniah. And many note the clear way in which Zechariah and Malachi have been shaped so as to achieve a twelve-book totality.

What Childs saw only provisionally, research on the Twelve has taken much further, extending his individual hermeneutical suggestions to the book as a whole. This does not erase

15. J. Jeremias, "Interrelationship," 185–86.

16. A. Cooper, "In Praise of Divine Caprice: The Significance of the Book of Jonah," in *Among the Prophets: Language, Image and Structure in the Prophetic Writings*, ed. P. R. Davies, JSOTSup 144 (Sheffield: JSOT Press, 1993), 159–63; P. Redditt, "Zechariah 9–14, Malachi, and the Redaction of the Book of the Twelve," in *Forming Prophetic Literature*, 264–65; Seitz, *Prophecy and Hermeneutics*, 146–49.

the individual witnesses but shows subsequent generations how to understand their comprehensive, composite understanding of history. My recent work gives further indication of the various accomplishments within the final form of the Twelve corpus. In that work, however, such accomplishments are assessed within the historical context of the emergence of introductions to the Prophets as discrete, popular treatments. Such textbooks were virtually unknown in the early nineteenth century because the larger canonical pressures assured that associations remained as they were conveyed in the final form of the "Law and Prophets" conceptuality. When defense of this conceptuality was urgently pressed, it was hard to find a way to honor the associations in the literature, given the rise of a powerful alternative sequential understanding. A canonical reading, however, values the associations and sees them as both intentional and theologically significant.

My purpose in the present chapter is to understand the significance of this "achievement of association" within the development of the canonical division of the Prophets, measured against efforts at arrangement and ordering occurring in the Law and in those books that came to be called the "Writings." We can see that this achievement is impressive both in its ambition and in its scope, and in that sense, there is nothing like it elsewhere in the canon. The closest analogy can be seen within the single book of Isaiah, where, unfortunately (or fortunately), we have nothing like the eleven seams between books to help us better understand Isaiah's compositional history, though I and others have sought to assess this dimension.

The way the Pentateuch reached final form has been the topic of much discussion in the formal study of the OT. What does a similar examination of the Prophets reveal? First of all, the Prophets clearly comprise different editorial processes, so that as a canonical division, it is a composite form. On the one hand, the Deuteronomistic history (DtrH) develops a four-book narrative account—composed of a wide variety of genres, previous traditions, and an array of available material—focused on an understanding of the destiny of the people of Israel, its leaders, its prophets, and its kings under the law of Moses. The achievement of this work, as with that of the Pentateuch (whose final book closes the Law and anticipates the Prophets), is enormous and need not be the subject of an extended discussion here. This history shows an Israel looking back to a book of the law as a finished reality and to a future known only in obedience to this law. Special attention is given to Israel's judges, prophets, and kings.[17]

The three major prophetic books are individual and very distinctive achievements. The order of the books was not fixed in the history of the Bible's reception; the Isaiah-Jeremiah-Ezekiel sequence is dominant but not the only one. The contrast with the Twelve is obvious because, among other differences, each of the Major Prophets is the length of the Twelve as a whole. That these three prophets are intended to sit next to the preceding four-book history is obvious both on historical grounds and in the light of superscriptions linking the three (and half the books of the Twelve) to the reigns of kings in Israel and Judah.[18] There are also significant reproductions of material from the History in the Three (e.g., the

---

17. Standard older treatments are M. Noth, *Überlieferungsgeschichtliche Studien: Die sammelnden und bearbeitenden Geschichtswerke im Alten Testaments*, 3rd ed. (Tübingen: Max Niemeyer, 1967); H. W. Wolff, "The Kerygma of the Deuteronomic Historical Work," in *The Vitality of Old Testament Traditions*, ed. W. Brueggemann and H. W. Wolff (Atlanta: John Knox, 1975); R. Nelson, *The Double Redaction of the Deuteronomistic History*, JSOTSup 18 (Sheffield: JSOT Press, 1981).

18. The prophetic superscriptions are often termed "Deuteronomistic."

Hezekiah narratives appear in 2 Kings 18–20 and Isa. 36–39; and 2 Kings 25 is reproduced as Jeremiah's conclusion).[19] At the precise middle point of the Twelve, we find the verse quoted by the elders of Moresheth in defense of Jeremiah. This dark death sentence over Zion—the first of its kind in the Twelve—is followed in Micah 4:1–5 by a text well known from Isaiah 2, which speaks of Zion's final vindication and exaltation for those who walk in God's ways (as Hosea's final appeal had it).[20] The Twelve are affiliated with the Three, and the Former Prophets with the Latter Prophets. The integrity of individual works and individual sections is clear, but so too are the efforts at an achievement of association.

The point to be stressed is that the hard work of creating a twelve-book prophetic achievement, such as we find in the Latter Prophets, is also happening in loose association with the History and the Three, such that a coherent prophetic corpus is emerging. The final editing of Malachi ("Remember the teaching of my servant Moses" [4:4]) is clearly meant as an inclusio, reaching back to Moses and Torah. But the concern with marriage and divorce, proper worship, and proper conduct in the face of forgetting God's ways or of despair over his command of history are matters the last book of the Twelve shares specifically with Hosea, the first book. The labor and the methods of association are prodigious and effective; there is nothing casual or happenstance about it.[21] The individual prophets of the Three and the Twelve are

19. C. Seitz, *Zion's Final Destiny: The Development of the Book of Isaiah; A Reassessment of Isaiah 36–39* (Minneapolis: Fortress, 1991).

20. The different ending of Micah, in my judgment, is a response to the appeal of Isaiah's distinctive ending, which in turn relates to the editorial hermeneutics of the Twelve, where the theme of the name of God and walking in his ways is prominent (see Van Leeuwen, note 11, above).

21. Something of the same effort at inclusio and recapitulation can be seen in the final chapters of Isaiah (65–66), and this has been the subject of extended

provided a history of prophecy in the DtrH that locates their activity in time-specific contexts and yet also seeks to understand prophecy as a uniform and coordinated phenomenon operating within the providential episodes of post-Mosaic leadership until the fall of Jerusalem and beyond.[22] Prophecy and law are inseparable. Prophecy belongs within a specific historical context (DtrH) and yet in the Twelve pushes beyond these horizons to an account of God's final intentions with Israel and the nations.

When one studies dislocations and adjustments in this association of the prophetic canon as they subsequently occur, two points stand out: (1) they are not uniform, and (2) they have taken the form either of attraction to a particular book (Ruth with Judges; Lamentations with Jeremiah) or of recasting the Former Prophets more generally (Chronicles may join Samuel and Kings but also Ezra-Nehemiah and Esther).

It is frequently argued that the order of our modern printed Bibles represents something like an alternative fourfold canonical order, in contrast to the tripartite form, going back to what is referred to, without much ado, as "the Septuagint." Sometimes this view is used to explain the final positioning of the prophetic division as leaning forward into the NT. Jews look back to Torah; Christians have a Bible that leans toward the new. Elijah is spoken of at the close of Malachi, and there he is, in the form of John the Baptist, at the beginning of the NT.

---

treatments. In the case of Malachi and Hosea, see John D. W. Watts, "A Frame for the Book of the Twelve: Hosea 1–3 and Malachi," in *Reading and Hearing the Book of the Twelve*, ed. J. Nogalski and M. Sweeney, SBLSymS 15 (Atlanta: SBL, 2000), 209–17.

22. C. Seitz, "Prophecy and History: The Book of the Twelve as History," in *Prophecy and Hermeneutics*, 189–219.

There are several problems with this view, one of which has already been intimated. A more likely explanation for the reordering of the tripartite is either the attraction of individual books to being ranged alongside neighbors or, more critically, an understanding of the Former Prophets as a distinct category (i.e., "historical" books) rather than as uniquely related to the Latter Prophets in one single division of Prophets following the Torah, an achievement I have been at pains to describe and to applaud. In my view, this logic is responsible for the dislocation of the tripartite, not any interest in having the Prophets "come last" for their own sake (which in almost all lists of antiquity does not happen). With the creation of a division of historical books and the association of Lamentations with Jeremiah, Ruth with Judges, and sometimes Job with "the books of Moses," the way was paved for the creation of a new category altogether, lyrical or poetic books, with the result that the Prophets were left to bring up the rear (in the lists where this occurs). But even this account cannot explain the wide diversity of orderings that later appeared. Writings, as we shall see, are individual witnesses, and their internal associations within this division are not significant, which means they can and will change position.

When we survey the lists from antiquity that diverge from the stable tripartite pattern of the MT, several critical features emerge:

1. None have Malachi or the Twelve in final position; Esther is more likely to be last.
2. The order varies widely.
3. The Twelve usually precedes Isaiah and the Major Prophets.

4. The Writings are not a distinct category analogous to Torah and Prophets, and the books change
position.[23]

What is the logic of this third division in contrast to the
Law and the Prophets? Barton's contention that we have
fixed "Mosaic" and a wide range of "non-Mosaic" books is
faulty on internal editorial (canonical) and developmental
(historical-critical) grounds, as we have been describing.
Moreover, on these same (historical-critical) terms, it is
clear that books of the Writings are both older and later
than the associations being accomplished in the Law and
the Prophets and so represent their own unique formation
history both as individual books and as an evolving library
of books.[24] Reference to "Law and Prophets" in the NT,
Ben Sira's prologue, the Praise of Famous Men, Tertullian,
and other places (e.g., Qumran) is sometimes accompanied
by mention of other writings. These books can be called

23. See note 1, above.
24. One thinks here of the lengthy and complex formation history of the Psalter,
Chronicles, and Job, among others. This makes Barton's theory of a subsequent
division of Writings based on chronological considerations faulty, alongside his
failure to see signs of affiliation and canonical order within the prophetic division itself. This can be said without prejudicing the question of whether in the
NT, for example, reference to the "Prophets" includes the Writings. It may well
be the case. But this "non-Mosaic" terminology, if that is what it is, leaves the
basic grammar of Law and Prophets in place, with the "Writings" simply included
alongside them as further "prophetic" witnesses with a different internal character.
Chronological factors are not relevant here. Daniel is excluded from the Prophets
not because he is too late (if that is the view held) but because Daniel is not part
of the achievement of the conjunction of the Deuteronomistic history, the Three,
and the Twelve. Also, Daniel is a "wise man," and in that consists his distinctive
"prophetic" role. A book such as Ruth may have been edited for its position in the
Writings (i.e., the "ideal wife" of Proverbs has been found) but also in order to be
associated with the juncture of Judges and Samuel. Job has a lengthy prehistory,
and the folktale retains all the color of the patriarchal (pre-Mosaic) age, but it
need not migrate out of the Writings for the point to be registered. Examples such
as this from the Writings could be multiplied.

prophetic in a generic sense, just as Moses or David can be called a prophet, but this happens alongside and not in competition with the Prophets represented in the Law and the Prophets.

Conclusions

As a way of setting forth the most likely explanation for the Writings as a distinct development vis-à-vis the achievement of association in the Law-Prophets conception, let me return to some of the rival views of canon and of the status of the OT at the time of the NT's formation. The status of the OT in NT times is regarded in one of three ways:

1. An authoritative collection of books, closed and in a fixed order (Zahn; Beckwith)
2. A collection of authoritative books (Bruce Metzger)
3. "A wide religious literature without definite bounds"— scripture but not canon (Sundberg)

The position I am defending here regards the OT as a defined collection of authoritative books (Law and Prophets) constituting a stable literary collection and an authorizing grammar. Accompanying this is a third category of writings that (a) could also subsequently be called prophetic in a general sense, (b) could in time, for reasons we can only conjecture, be inserted into the canonical Prophets without thereby disturbing the grammar of "the Law and the Prophets," (c) may not have been closed and in fixed order at the time of the NT, and (d) were relatively stable nonetheless and were differentiated in some fashion from the books later termed "Apocrypha," which are not quoted/

cited in the NT as Scripture but are only alluded to in minimal ways.[25]

Albert Sundberg is the most influential name associated with modern canon studies that seek to distinguish canonicity as a late matter of closing (the third view listed above). In the area of NT canon formation, Sundberg demolished the idea of a stable Alexandrian canon adopted by Christians over against the evolving Hebrew canon. He has built his views upon a decisive conception that stands in opposition to that of Harnack, Zahn, von Campenhausen, and others. According to Sundberg, the OT was not "canon" but rather "scripture" at the time of the NT—"a wide religious literature without definite bounds." He asserts, "The Christian church did not receive a canon of scripture but scripture on its way to a definitive canon in Judaism." This view has been accepted and extended by John Barton, who does not see order, closure, or delimitation as characteristic of the OT in NT times.[26] A recent treatment by Craig Allert has given the view fresh if surprising popularization, though Allert's chief interest is in the rule of faith and the development of NT canonical writings.[27]

25. To a certain extent, my earlier position reflected a different set of interlocutors. My worry in the present study is hermeneutical. Requiring too strict an account of fixity will likely ask canon to bear a weight that is not appropriate to it and may misunderstand the difference between the Law and the Prophets and the Writings in their canonical logic. See my "Two Testaments and the Failure of One Tradition History," in *Figured Out: Typology and Providence in Christian Scripture* (Louisville: Westminster John Knox, 2001), 35–47.

26. See note 6 of chap. 2, above. Already at Qumran, the Twelve are in a clearly fixed order, and the significance of this has been noted recently by Francis Watson along with many others. According to Watson, Habakkuk's sense is a function of its relationship to this stable order. This is not something "read into" Habakkuk after the fact, anymore than the editing of Amos and Hosea is extrinsic to them as individual or associated witnesses (so Jeremias). The same is true of Isaiah as a single witness and of the Deuteronomistic history.

27. Craig D. Allert, *A High View of Scripture? The Authority of the Bible and the Formation of the New Testament Canon*, Evangelical *Ressourcement* (Grand Rapids: Baker Academic, 2007).

In contrast to Sundberg's claims, I would state the matter this way: The Christian church received authoritative scriptures in definitive form (Law and Prophets), whose tripartite order (as in later Judaism) was there in clear and emergent form to begin with but whose outer limit was not established definitively and formally until later, under specific constraints. But even this formal closing was not so much an imposition as a clarification that what was received was stable: a grammar of Law and Prophets, to which was added a third category of Writings, whose number and order was by then a more settled matter. The following chapter will deal with the unique accomplishment represented by this third division. By way of anticipation, several things should be said here so that the question of the status of the OT at the time of the NT can be sharpened.

A later, more formal "closing of the canon" in Judaism would not prevent the church from receiving additional writings or representing the internal orders of the scriptures of Israel in a variety of ways, but neither did it prevent the church from acknowledging the authority and revelatory pressure of these writings prior to their formal closing, whether their closing in Judaism or in the church. In my view, the rule of faith in the early church fathers is a correlating of the gospel with the stable and authoritative claims of the scriptures of Israel, seen now as a first testament and crucial foundational witness. However, the disparity in the way sequence and order would be manifested in the church indicates that the adjustments were not theologically/hermeneutically motivated but were haphazard and incidental (*pace* Sweeney). Consequently, this order cannot serve as an argument against using the order as preserved in the MT as a vehicle for recovering the "canonical text" (so Childs). Following this logic, the hermeneutical and theological achievement of the tripartite is honored, especially in the retention of the "Law and the Prophets," which finds widespread usage in the NT as a term to refer to the scriptures of Israel. Adjustments in the Christian lists should be understood as just that.

As a way forward in the canonical impasse, John Barton in the 1990 Hulsean Lectures adopted the criterion of use and density of citation as a mark of "canonicity" or its authoritative equivalent on Barton's terms.[28] The NT use of the OT, however, is determined by the subject matter appropriate to its scope, claims, and intentionality, and this says nothing about the authority and formal logic (Law and Prophets) of the writings the church received. Indeed, it is because the notion of reception, acknowledgment, and deference is held hostage by Barton and Sundberg to an idea of fixed and closed canonical lists that confusion has entered in, resulting in Barton's using a functional logic to determine "canon" on new terms.

The fatal step came earlier, when Barton failed to see the logic of "Law and Prophet" as a sign of early canon formation. Instead he spoke of (a) Mosaic writings and (b) all other writings.[29] He judged the use of the general terminology "prophet" (as applicable to any non-Mosaic book) as evidence that there was no formal category "prophet" from which such a generalized use was derived. "Writings" can

28. John Barton, *The Spirit and the Letter: Studies in the Biblical Canon* (London: SPCK, 1997).

29. See John Barton, "The Law and the Prophets," in *The Oracles of God: Perceptions of Ancient Prophecy in Israel after the Exile* (London: Darton, Longman, & Todd, 1986), 35–94. The subtitle of the book has the potential of detaching the historical and canonical realities of "the Prophets," such as we are describing it here (Deuteronomistic history, the Three, and the Twelve), from its historical footings and moving toward *Wirkungsgeschichte*, where "prophet" has a more imprecise status in the nature of the material under discussion.

indeed be referred to as prophetic works, just as Moses can be called a prophet on occasion, but this detracts nothing from the widespread and formal appeal to "Law and Prophets" as a clear conceptuality and grammar in the emergent scriptural legacy.[30] Sundberg confused the matter further by speaking of "scriptures" as distinct from "canon" and then using the former term to designate a literature sufficiently vague that both terms became redefined. Yet Tertullian can speak of the "Law and Prophets" as constituting a "volume one" of Christian writings. By this he means the Law and Prophets as we understand it on historical and canonical terms (i.e., Moses and the Former and Latter Prophets) but also the wider collection of scriptural writings, whose authority is not dependent either on a single interior order (so the eventual recasting of Prophets and Writings divisions) or on the precise delimitation that Sundberg requires for the notion of canon to make sense on his terms.

The Writings: Transition

Crucial to any account of the authority of the OT at the time of the NT is understanding the logic of the "Law and the Prophets," on the one hand, and the very different logic of "Writings," on the other. In the first instance, "Writings" are not formed so as to find the associative status within the scope of their respective division that, ultimately, will accrue to the Law and the Prophets. Writings derive their logic, canonically, from being external to, independent of, but in loose association with, not one another, but the in-

---

30. S. Chapman (*The Law and the Prophets: A Study in Old Testament Canon Formation*, FAT 27 [Tübingen: Mohr Siebeck, 2000]) has done a good job of emphasizing this point, and he is now followed by Steins and others.

dividual books or mature arrangements of the Law and the Prophets. Any association they have with one another within the Writings—and here the contrast with Law and Prophets is clear—is a much weaker form of relationship. This means the books can and do migrate in subsequent listings in the Christian church, even as within Judaism senses of internal association are achieved by establishing stable orderings of the Writings.

In canonical terms, this means that the Writings are books with a higher degree of individuality within the third section, and they find association with books in the Law and Prophets either useful for or indispensable to their logic. This also means that the precise number of such writings, and so the notion of closure so highly prized in the logic of Barton and Sundberg, is not so crucial as these scholars maintain, at least for the purpose of assessing the authority of the received books of the OT by the church. In time, the Writings stabilize in Judaism, while in the Christian church they tend to migrate and find a wide variety of new associations. In the next chapter, we will explain how this happens. In either the Jewish or Christian context, however, the authority of the individual writings presupposes a prior stability and logic in the books of the Law and the Prophets. In a way that anticipates the development of a two-testament Christian Scripture, what the Writings judge to be true of the Law and the Prophets, so also the NT judges to be true both of the Law and the Prophets and of this third category of books, books it can happily term prophetic, so natural is the field of association binding them all.

Efforts to read theological or historical significance into the divergent orders of books in ancient lists are both misleading and without a logic attested in Christian reception history.

Even the debate between Jerome and Augustine finally found resolution in a theory of double inspiration, and nothing in the debate suggests that different listings figured crucially into it. It is the nature of the Writings, as individual books without strong internal association, to migrate toward other books with which they have intentional literary and theological affiliation, and indeed in some cases it appears that the books that tend to migrate may have editorial features that allow them without difficulty to function both inside and outside the Writings.

In the next chapter, we will see why the achievement of the tripartite organization is the vehicle through which to assess what Childs called the canonical OT. This is so, even though Childs acknowledged that different orders emerged over time in the Christian church, including, most obviously, the conventions of modern printed Bibles. The point is subtle and belongs inside the logic of what he called "the search for the Christian Bible."

Canon and History

The tripartite format is precisely a theological *assessment* of history. This is not the same thing as a sequential or developmental account, which in its fashion has been described as "the historical account." This is especially clear when one tries to understand the logic of the Minor Prophets, which lies at the heart and foundation of the prophetic division of the canon. These books are not in "historical" order, but in the order in which they are presented, they intend to give a theological account of history.

By its very resistance to organization along strictly diachronic lines based on the author's location, original situation-in-life, and the like, the tripartite preserves an account of history that is more than lining up a reconstruction of the sequence of intentions. The Law and the Prophets is an achievement of association that locates the major episodes of God's work with Israel in time and space and allows that speech and action to overtake and orient subsequent generations so that they may learn God's ways and walk in them. The individual books in the Writings pick up the dynamic available in the Law and the Prophets and seek to extend it in specific ways (e.g., David and Psalms, Solomon and Wisdom, the patriarchs and Job, and the Chronicler's account of prophetic history).

Finally, a quick word about the NT. Another chapter would be needed to develop these brief closing observations; however, I have undertaken discussion of this issue in a forthcoming book, *The Character of Christian Scripture: Canon and the Rule of Faith.*

Recent scholarship's argument for a "diverse body of literature without order or arrangement" removes the OT from a significant place in the formation of Christian theology in the early church, where by means of a rule of faith the confession of Jesus as Lord was correlated with the OT. The New was related to a stable and privileged Old and gained its force precisely because of this connection with the Old. In this manner, the way was paved for the formation of a NT on analogy with the received scriptures of Israel, the Law and the Prophets, which came in time to be called the OT. The notion of "a diverse body of literature without order or arrangement" does not do justice to this dynamic. It threatens to remove the OT as crucial in the activity, mission, and self-understanding of Jesus Christ and as a key ingredient in the actual formation of the NT as canon.

The influence of the OT consists in more than a haphazard utilization of OT passages for proof-text purposes. It constitutes more than mere background material or exciting intellectual milieu drawn upon for a narrative world within which Jesus understands his mission. It is more than a prominent exegetical resource that Paul and other NT writers draw from and that merits our attention and emulation. In its formal and material givenness, the Law and the Prophets pattern has influenced the formal and material development of the NT as canon. Here Deuteronomy's function finds a correlate in John's relationship to the Synoptics, which shows concern for the post-Easter appropriation of the heart of Jesus's message by the apostolic generation inspired by the Holy Spirit, who are enabled to remember Jesus's words and to understand the witness to Jesus accomplished by the OT. The individual and associative aspects of the Twelve find analogies in the Pauline Letter collection, where both the individual and the associative aspects must be carefully handled. Hebrews, the Catholic Epistles, and Revelation occupy a similar hermeneutical position to the Writings of the OT canon.

A goodly fellowship of the prophets lies at the heart of OT canon formation. It ought then to come as no surprise that the One God of Israel, whose Son's work was in accordance with the Scriptures, would oversee as well a goodly fellowship of apostles, the result being the creation of a NT canon whose subject matter and material form are influenced by the scriptures of Israel. These are the Scriptures with which the life, death, and resurrection of Jesus are said to be in accord. These two witnesses would in time form the one Christian Scripture of the post-apostolic church, among whose number we are counted, having been brought to faith by their testimony.

4

The Accomplishment of the Writings

It is now possible to undertake a study of the accomplishment of the third division of the canon, the Writings. We have already indicated the general position that the Writings, as a division, do not intend the same kind of accomplishment as that represented in the Prophets. Unlike the Law or the Prophets, the Writings do not exhibit a concern to order the individual works in any theologically significant way. The Writings are individual achievements of association and as such are read in conjunction with the basic grammar of the scriptures of Israel, that is, the Law and the Prophets. The second division is not a loose collection of books of diverse origins; neither is it composed merely of any non-Mosaic book that fails to find its place in the stable canonical foundation of the Law. Deuteronomy's logic is crucial in this regard: it has been severed from what will become the Former Prophets subdivision in order to assist in the proper interpretation of this now dual witness. In the words of Georg Steins, "There is no canonized Torah without *Nebiim* because one cannot imagine the Torah without interpretation." The formal logic is "Moses, the original prophet, and the *successio mosaico*, which guarantees an authentic interpretation" of the foundational revelation.[1]

The previous chapter made clear the sophisticated effort at internal cohesion and affiliation evident in the prophetic division. Pivotal in this regard is the book of the Twelve. The cross-references and duplications of material from Former and Latter Prophets, and from the Twelve and the Three, indicate the unique character of the accomplishment of the Prophets as a canonical division. By contrast, the Writings are a diverse collection.[2] Several of the writings are clearly older than the processes that brought together the prophetic division and the individual witnesses of that division.[3] This

1. From his unpublished Vienna address (see note 15 of the introduction, above).

2. Steins speaks of two distinct processes. He writes, "Concept (2) can be found in the 'writings.' It is of great significance to stress the formal difference between the 'writings' and the 'Torah and Prophets': The 'writings' totally differ from the preceding canonical parts. They must be considered as a loose compilation of books which are not kept together from inside but from outside: i.e., the popular image of the 'book collection' and 'library' is an inadequate description of the canon as a whole as it fails to illustrate the various ways of cohesion. The Hellenistic concept of the library is realized in the 'writings' which do not pursue the goal of gathering world knowledge (wisdom), but which predominately seek to provide a genre-wise multi-faceted ideal-anthology of high quality as evidence of cultural equality" (12).

3. This calls into question the position of Barton, who holds chronological factors to be the reason for a subsequent "Writings" division. It is difficult to see how one could hold this view unless driven to it by a one-after-the-other model of closure in the subsections of the canon. Barton writes, "What is certain is that Judaism eventually came to recognize a third category, limiting 'the Prophets' to the four history books . . . and the four 'prophetic' books proper . . . and placing all other non-Pentateuchal books into a category called blandly the Writings. The basis for the division seems to be mainly chronological: the Writings are the later books of the Hebrew Bible" (J. Barton, *The Making of the Christian Bible*

means that they existed independently as individual works, and no effort was made to include them within the developing canon of Law and Prophets. No effort was necessary, on the assumption that the character of the Writings as individual works would be grasped as it is. In some cases, as with the Psalter, we can see evidence of a major effort at internal development and association within the limits of the book itself.[4] This was no small accomplishment for the Psalter. It resulted in a five-book collection, with proper introduction and conclusion and a highly sophisticated system of cross-reference, superscripting, and midrashic associations with other works of the canon.

Many of the writings function as individual works with a field of association that links them to the logic of Law and Prophets and not to one another within the division of the Writings itself. David, torah, temple, and covenant are all themes of the Psalter whose wider logic is asserted in the Law and the Prophets and merely assumed as available for cross-reference. The internal logic of the Writings is not associative but serial. A similar point has been made by Gerald Sheppard in regard to what he called "wisdom as a hermeneutical construct"—that is, efforts to shape individual writings associated with Wisdom so as to relate them clearly to the grammar and logic of the Law and the

---

[London: Darton, Longman & Todd, 1997], 42). Barton almost perfectly replicates the kind of logic we are here concerned with, terming the second division "four history books" and "prophetic" books proper. Is Lamentations later than Ezekiel? Proverbs later than 2 Kings? Ruth later than Isaiah or Malachi? Psalms later than the book of the Twelve in finished form? Song of Songs datable at all? Chronological criteria are not straightforward when one deals with the complex canonical shaping of books and moves beyond the "original works" logic that majors in chronological factors.

4. The secondary literature is wide ranging. See my brief summary in *Word without End* (Waco: Baylor University Press, 2004), 150–67.

Prophets.[5] The conclusion to Ecclesiastes is a good example of this.[6]

This view of the Writings does not itself rule out stable orders or sequencing of the books, but it understands such arrangements on different terms than we see in the Law or the prophetic division. The lack of a fixed order, a fixed number, or something amounting to closure would be immaterial to the basic canonical authority that accrues to the scriptures of Israel in the form of what could be termed a "core canon."[7] That authority is a given in the Law and the Prophets. It furthermore misunderstands the character of the Writings to demand a form of closure or fixed internal arrangement that is at odds with the logic of this particular section as its own unique achievement.

The unique character of the Writings as Writings also explains why these books have migrated in lists that can be consulted in the history of the Christian church or even in Josephus, for example. This migrating was not intended to disturb the fundamental grammar of the Law and the Prophets. Its haphazard character, as represented in divergent

5. G. Sheppard, *Wisdom as a Hermeneutical Construct: A Study of the Sapientializing of the Old Testament*, BZAW 151 (Berlin: de Gruyter, 1980).

6. Noting the unique character of this division, Childs made this summary comment in *Introduction to the Old Testament as Scripture* (Philadelphia: Fortress, 1979), 503: "The major theological implications to be drawn from this evidence is that the collection of material into a third division, which supplemented the Law and the Prophets, performed a significant canonical role for Judaism. The canonical shaping left its impact in fixing the scope of the section and in the shaping of individual books. However, the sequence of the books within the canonical division had little significance and no normative order was ever established by the synagogue." Childs notes the possible exception of the Megilloth.

7. J. Collins ("Before the Canon: Scriptures in Second Temple Judaism," in *Old Testament Interpretation: Past, Present, and Future; Essays in Honor of Gene M. Tucker*, ed. J. L. Mays, D. L. Petersen, and K. H. Richards [Nashville: Abingdon, 1995], 225–41) speaks of the centrality of Torah and the acknowledgment of a second category of writings whose total number is less fixed in the period before Josephus (232).

listings, warns against thinking that a different overall theological statement was intended by orders that differ from the tripartite. There is too much variety in the lists for that to be the case. Even the reference to a fourfold order, which we have adopted as shorthand, is not some sort of hard option presenting itself over against the tripartite. Rather, it exists as a convention in modern English printed Bibles, one that does not point to any single or even dominant family of earlier exemplars.[8]

We can now turn to several theories that have taken up the question of the character of the Writings, their order, number, and arrangement. Basic to them all is a rejection of the idea that there is some linear development of the canon, with one section closing only after the preceding one was settled.[9] The Law and the Prophets did not develop in this way, and neither did the Writings, which as individual works both preceded and followed the core canonical accomplishment. The linear view made closure so crucial that it *even sought to retroject it back into two prior phases so as to enhance this view of the cruciality of closure and exclusion for the meaning of canonical authority.* From the earliest point we can track them, the origins of canon formation are far more complicated and point to reciprocal and deeply cross-affiliated relationships. In the book of the Twelve, it is likely that Amos and Hosea, the first two books, never circulated independently, and the association of them produced a model that took hold immediately and never ceased until the production of the Twelve was complete.

8. It may be traceable to later developments in the Vulgate's history.

9. The work of Stephen Chapman (*The Law and the Prophets: A Study in Old Testament Canon Formation*, FAT 27 [Tübingen: Mohr Siebeck, 2000]) is crucial in establishing this point. The Law and the Prophets emerge through a reciprocal editing process and not one after the other.

Indeed, it is questionable whether individual books of the Twelve had much of an individual life. Jonah's conclusion has been argued to lie outside of its literary limits. The final three books are clearly connected to one another and to the preceding witnesses (e.g., Haggai/Zechariah in Ezra 5:1; the repetition of *maśśā'* in Zech. 9:1; 12:1; and Mal. 1:1; Zechariah's reference to "former prophets" in 1:4 and 7:7; Mal. 4:4–5 and Torah-Moses and Former Prophets–Elijah). The violence decried at Habakkuk's beginning is seen clearly in Nahum, which precedes it. Obadiah has been reckoned a "virtual commentary on Amos," and I have argued for the significance of Zephaniah following Habakkuk and of Joel intruding between Hosea and Amos.[10] This brief description of the order and arrangement of the Minor Prophets stands in contrast to the principles at work in the Writings.

Before turning to theories for the existence, order, and scope of the Writings, a word about them as individual works is needed in order to provide a working conception. It will also serve as an overview to a division whose contents have become obscured by alternative arrangements. Psalms, Proverbs, and Job are clearly large-scale independent works. As such, they resemble the great prophetic collections of Isaiah, Jeremiah, and Ezekiel, whose sequence is also of minor significance. The book of Daniel, the subject of much discussion due to its migration in other listings, describes its protagonist as a wisdom figure and does not apply the term "prophet" to him. Von Rad correctly saw apocalyptic as deriving from

10. See the newer work on the Twelve from Collins, A. Schart, Nogalski, Jeremias, Rendtorff, Van Leeuwen, Cooper, and others and my discussion in C. Seitz, *Prophecy and Hermeneutics: Toward a New Introduction to the Prophets*, STI (Grand Rapids: Baker Academic, 2007).

wisdom circles, and so Daniel's location in the Writings is completely logical.[11]

A pattern of migration to the prophetic books is explicable on the same general terms as for Ruth, Lamentations, Chronicles, and Ezra-Nehemiah. In each of these cases, there was a decision to make explicit by literary rearrangement a form of association that the Writings were content to accomplish more implicitly and generally. Daniel makes explicit reference to Jeremiah's prediction, and it is crucial to its presentation. Moving Daniel next to Jeremiah might make that relationship clearer, but only if the logic of the Writings as a third canonical division was not grasped sufficiently. A collection of Solomonic works, different than the Psalter but also reflecting a royal imprimatur, explains the loose association intended for Proverbs, Song of Songs, and Ecclesiastes. Such an imprimatur creates a field of association without thereby diminishing the achievement of the works as independent books. This association remains intact in divergent orders such as that of modern printed Bibles, which introduces a category of poetical or lyrical books, or the modern scholarly conception of "Wisdom literature."

The logic of non-tripartite orders was not based on a desire to create a theological statement of great significance, though this is sometimes asserted. The final location of the Prophets is actually not widespread in Christian lists and does not exist in the form that would popularly lead to the idea of an alleged eschatalogizing view of Judaism in contrast to a more historical or torah-centric one.[12] The impetus for re-categorizing stems instead from confusion over the logic of the prophetic division, which contains books of a histori-

---

11. G. von Rad, *Wisdom in Israel* (Nashville: Abingdon, 1972).
12. M. Sweeney (see note 26, chap. 1).

cal character. This led to the introduction of "historical" as a category unto itself and caused the migration of Ruth, Chronicles, Ezra-Nehemiah, and Esther. A similar associating instinct moved Lamentations next to Jeremiah and moved Daniel into the Prophets. It had nothing to do with divisions being open or closed. Rather, it made explicit associations that the Writings were content to leave implicit, thus guarding the crucial character of the Law and the Prophets in their material bipartite form.

Here I can only briefly assess the peculiar achievement of the Megilloth within the Writings. On the face of it, this collection of five smaller books could represent a stronger instinct toward association, which I have said characterizes only the Law and the Prophets. Persuasive explanations for the present fivefold order have been given, and these explanations do not turn on notions of liturgical usage, though they may explain such a development. But even this effort at association did not prevent the books from migrating, and perhaps it would be better to search for editorial moves at work within these five books that enable their present arrangement in the Writings as well as their migration and re-association.[13] The Leningrad order of the Megilloth seems to have its own special character within the Ketubim. Proverbs describes the ideal wife, which Ruth is. Song of Songs describes the bliss of love and can apply to Boaz and Ruth by juxtaposition. Ecclesiastes stipulates the limits to pleasure

---

13. Ruth is critical in this regard. It appears to be edited for two positions. Ruth represents the solution to the dilemma of Judges ("there was no king in Israel; all the people did what was right in their own eyes" [17:6; 21:25]), and its opening rubric locates its point in this temporal frame of reference. The final genealogy links backward to Genesis and forward to King David, and the song of Hannah picks up the theme of hope for David in the opening chapters of 1 Samuel. Yet the links to Proverbs are equally compelling, as that book describes the "woman of valor," and Boaz confirms that he has found her.

in physical, intellectual, and commercial life and emphasizes the dangers of seeking permanence through earthly profit in these areas. Lamentations applies the fate of the individual to the fate of the nation as a whole, and Esther shows the other side of this, in positive terms.

The final book or books of the Writings may also have special significance. This of course forces us to revisit the question of the scope and fixed/closed character of the division as a whole. I have not wanted to make this issue fundamental for canonical authority because it tends to prioritize the aspect of final closure to the detriment of organic hermeneutical moves toward association and interpretation, which track the formation of the canonical divisions from their earliest phases through to the end phases. Moreover, such a view tends to suggest that closing was crucial for each individual division, although we have seen that the Law and the Prophets, the primary grammar of the OT, developed in reciprocal relationship with one another and not on these terms.

There have been efforts to describe a stable (or relatively stable) order, number, and arrangement of the Writings, whose character is settled well prior to the development of the NT. Beckwith has drawn attention to the NT reference to prophetic martyrs from Abel to Zechariah to argue for a stable Hebrew canon closing with Chronicles.[14] Zahn used a criterion of citation in the church fathers, contrasting this with the way NT writings were referred to, in order to claim a stable Hebrew canon at the time of the NT.[15] In more general terms, von Campenhausen insisted that we understand the early church as operating self-consciously with a sole He-

14. R. T. Beckwith, *The Old Testament Canon of the New Testament Church* (Grand Rapids: Eerdmans, 1985).

15. T. Zahn, *Geschichte des neutestamentlichen Kanons*, 2 vols. (Leipzig: Hinrichs'sche Buchhandlung, 1888–92).

brew Scripture in order to preach Christ and doing so quite efficiently while a second canonical witness was only slowly emerging and gaining a canonical authority on the basis of, and on analogy with, this antecedent witness.[16] In these latter two cases, the stability of the Writings was assumed and not argued, since the question of precise order and arrangement was not as crucial as the overall stability and consolidated character of the witness, especially as one could observe this in citations of the church fathers.

Space allows mention of only a few specialized examinations of the Writings. One of these entails the observation about the tripartite canon as a whole and the symmetrical way the books of Torah and Former Prophets are balanced by Latter Prophets and Writings.[17] Dividing the tripartite format in half like this produces two sections of almost precisely equal length (150,000 words); such symmetry can work only with the Hebrew Bible in tripartite form, and only when Daniel is left out. This also results in a twenty-three-book total, which corresponds to the number of letters of the Hebrew alphabet at the time, the middle of the fourth century BC. The complete book of Daniel is later than this, but its inclusion is accomplished well before the Christian era.

16. H. von Campenhausen, *The Formation of the Christian Bible* (London: Adam & Charles Black, 1972). Compare as well Harnack's observation: "[Lessing] perceived that the New Testament as a book and as the recognised fundamental document of the Christian religion originated in the Church. But Lessing did not recognise that the Book from the moment of its origin freed itself from all conditions of its birth, and at once claimed to be an entirely independent and unconditioned authority. This was indeed only possible because the book at once took its place beside the Old Testament, which occupied a position of absolute and unquestionable independence because it was more ancient than the Church" (A. Harnack, *Bible Reading in the Early Church* [London: Williams & Norgate, 1912], 145).

17. D. N. Freeman, "The Symmetry of the Hebrew Bible," *Studia theologica* 46 (1992): 83–108.

The details of the argument need not detain us here. There is, however, one specific use of the theory that points to the significance, not so much of a fixed internal order within the Writings, but of the final book or books as these are provided in a serial listing. It stands to reason that significance would be attached to whichever book or books stood last in the Writings. Many studies have shown that similar editorial concern is evident in Deuteronomy and Malachi, which stand at the seams of Torah and Prophets and of Prophets and Writings, respectively.[18] Malachi relates the entire prophetic division to Moses and torah observance, even as it constitutes an *inclusio* with Hosea, the first book of the Twelve. The conclusion of the Writings, moreover, has significance not just for the single division but also for the tripartite canon as a whole. The internal order was not as significant in the Writings as it was in the prophetic division, which may have led to increased concern with the beginning and closing books of the division.[19]

It is likely that the question of the finality of the Writings was especially challenging. Building on the consensus view that Daniel is a late book and, more controversially, may disrupt something of an achievement of symmetry in the canonical Hebrew Bible as a whole, John Sailhamer has offered an intriguing set of observations.[20] Examining two traditions

18. Blenkinsopp, Sheppard, Childs, and Chapman emphasize this.

19. I am grateful to Paul Raabe for pointing out the significance of the placement of Chronicles first in Leningradensis (which is not reproduced in *BHS*). Not only does this make chronological and comprehensive sense in the Writings division (since Chronicles reproduces a history from creation to anticipated temple restoration), but in the codex in question it also creates an *inclusio* with the edict of Cyrus at the beginning and at the end (with Ezra 1:1).

20. John H. Sailhamer, "Biblical Theology and the Composition of the Hebrew Bible," in *Biblical Theology: Retrospect and Prospect*, ed. Scott J. Hafemann (Downers Grove, IL: InterVarsity; Leicester, UK: Apollos, 2002), 25–37.

of Hebrew listings—*Baba Batra* and Codex B19a (the earliest complete medieval manuscript)—he notes that one has Chronicles in final position, the other has Ezra-Nehemiah. If Ezra-Nehemiah follows Daniel, whose individual character has been noted, the edict of Cyrus may be taken as the true fulfillment of Daniel's prediction of seventy years times seven, which in such an arrangement becomes an eccentric prediction. The force of Daniel is thus domesticated by an editorial interpretation that construes exile as ending with the return and the rebuilding of the temple. If Chronicles follows Daniel, however, a different effect results. Chronicles ends with the decree of Cyrus and offers a more polished form of it than Ezra-Nehemiah. This allows the prediction of Daniel to stand and its fulfillment to be realized when the LORD brings about the return to Jerusalem intimated in hopeful ways by the final line of Chronicles: "Whoever is among you of all his people, may the LORD his God be with him! Let him go up" (2 Chron. 36:23). Sailhamer prefers this latter order.

My interest in this intriguing set of alternatives and in the significance of their differing orders is somewhat different from Sailhamer's, however. It shows that the order of the Writings *was under negotiation or open to recasting* even, or especially, at the point of their possible/anticipated conclusion. This is true even if one disputes Sailhamer's conjectures about the significance of the two different orders, not to mention the order we see in Leningradensis, with Chronicles first. He wishes to see the ending with Chronicles as especially meaningful in light of the wider Christian Bible with its subsequent NT canonical witness. Both he and Freedman, for different reasons, hold relatively conservative dates for the stabilization of the Hebrew Bible. But of course, strictly speaking, "stabilization" is the wrong term if it is used to rule out the existence of different orders and of books whose position is being negotiated, notably in the third division of the canon, the Writings.

For our purposes, what is notable is the way in which re-arrangements are both possible in a collection such as the Writings and consistent with their special character over against the Law and the Prophets. Subsequent to whatever is going on with Daniel, Ezra-Nehemiah, and Chronicles, we know that Ruth and Lamentations can migrate and join with Judges and Jeremiah, respectively. There is a certain naturalness in this. In time, moreover, the Former Prophets can admit Chronicles, Ezra-Nehemiah, and Ezra into their ranks. Other books emerge in a new canonical grouping ("po-etic books" appearing either after historically arranged ones or bringing up the rear with additional deuterocanonical books, as in Sinaiticus and Alexandrinus) or are randomly relocated to various positions in the listings we know from Christian sources. But all that is happening in the Writings is consistent with the character of these books and the divi-sion in which they are found. The same is not true of the Law and the Prophets.

In an address given at the 2007 international meeting of the Society of Biblical Literature in Vienna, Georg Steins surveyed work on the OT canon and drew attention to several recent accounts that took seriously the role of the Ketubim in canon formation. Albert de Pury believed that the Writings emerged as a distinct category of books in the late biblical period in order to address the challenge of life in Diaspora. They showed that Israel, like its neighbors, had a library of literature addressing more general themes than the Law and the Prophets. On a different tack, Karel van der Toorn, in a probably unlikely alliance with Childs, questioned the priority given to closure in accounts of canonical texts and collections. Steins's own view builds on these studies. He sees the Writings as like a classical library. The basic grammar of the OT remains the Law and the Prophets, and these works operate in conjunction with that grammar.

The conclusions I have reached about the Writings are consistent with these recent studies. The Writings are a distinctive category. The character of their internal arrangement is different in kind from the Prophets and evolved in distinction to the accomplishment of association noted in the prophetic division. One finds major independent collections (Psalms, Job, Proverbs) whose ordering is according to loose principles of association, not unlike Isaiah, Jeremiah, and Ezekiel. Daniel is a unique work of wisdom circles and likely the latest of these compositions in its final form. The Megilloth show some signs of intentional association, due probably to their shared size and the way the themes they address are capable of linkage, but this linkage is not so strong that it cannot be rearranged, as in the liturgical order of *BHS* or in the migrating decisions of other listings, which are far more diverse than the convention of modern printed Bibles (e.g., Esther is often last). Chronicles is a special book, reflecting a kind of prophetic contemporizing of the former historical activity in the age of prophets and kings. It is a prophetic book according to its own species, appropriate to its location in the Writings and offering a comprehensive picture from Adam to the eventual return to Jerusalem (a new Eden?). Its placement alongside 1 and 2 Kings dampened, if not blunted altogether, the specific prophetic character of both works, turning a Former Prophet into history and then reinforcing the decision by ranging Chronicles next to it in a new category with Ezra-Nehemiah and Esther. The accomplishment of the prophetic division was thereby obscured, and the pivotal role of Chronicles as a Writing was likewise affected.

We have accepted the reality of migration and divergent orders in the Ketubim and have sought to account for it through a careful assessment of the character that marks off this division. My chief point is that efforts to have a totally stabilized (and closed) Ketubim have placed something of an unrealistic burden on otherwise maximal accounts of the canonical authority of the "OT" at the time of the NT. This does not deny that there is stability, but this stability does not preclude shuffling and migrating. The "Writings" are sufficiently individual works, sufficiently deferential to the core canon, and sufficiently diverse and varied as works that the NT need not refer to them as a distinct canonical unit in order for them to be fully a part of a stable "OT," albeit in shifting orders. The NT shorthand "Moses and the Prophets" is not an attempt to describe a totality or provide canonical precision for later scholarship but simply a way to describe "the OT" in a compact way. Adding up references in the NT and early church fathers to the various books of the Bible, including the Writings, supports this conclusion, for the Writings are cited (especially the Psalms). But the chief problem here is that subsequent selection is governed by the subject matter under discussion and not by the need to provide a comprehensive account of all antecedently authoritative texts.

The very fact that it is possible to see divergent endings in the Writings or to reconstruct plausible cases of this is again consistent with the character of the division. But there is also a practical matter of relevance. The kind of association accomplished in the Law and in the prophetic divi sion is of such a character that it does not require a codex for reinforcement. Already at Qumran, twelve individual prophetic books appear in a fixed and stable sequence. Ben Sira likewise supports the Twelve as a collection, not just as individual works, though the sequencing required Qumran for corroboration. The Writings may well have gravitated toward sequential stabilization simply due to the nature of the matter (randomness is awkward when making secondary references to them), but because they are individual works, different in kind from the Law or the Prophets, sequence was not a crucial issue. The same could in theory be said of their total number. The challenge probably emerged in the context of determining which book should occupy the final position, since its significance would in time be obvious. The same might have been true of the initial book, but far less so, because it was the final book of the Writings that would become the final book of the scriptures of Israel. However, it is difficult to do more than speculate in the manner of Sailhamer about the effect of arrangements of three books— Daniel, Chronicles, and Ezra-Nehemiah. If the priority of the canonical Hebrew Bible was the Law and the Prophets, as I have argued, the significance of what would become the last book of the canon would still have to find its logic in relationship to that fundamental grammar.

One final word about hermeneutics and canon. In a recent work, Craig Allert has revisited OT canon formation in order to diminish the criterion of von Campenhausen and Harnack concerning the formation of the NT canon. Following Sundberg and Barton, Allert disputes that the distinction between works cited with the phrase "it is written" as opposed to allusions of various kinds can be used as a way to determine, by contrast with canonical OT citations, the authoritative writings of the NT. He is chiefly concerned with the NT and questions of canon formation on that side of the Christian Bible. This leads him to a robust reliance on what he calls the rule of faith in the early church as determinative for the authority of NT books. This he contrasts with traditional evangelical reliance on inspiration, apostlicity, and the like—a so-called high view of Scripture—which he sets out to question.[21]

As Allert assesses the NT's development and canonical status in an attempt to eliminate a criterion of citation ("it is written"), which he, following Sundberg, judges to be inadequate, the OT's canonical influence falls entirely out of discussion. The result is that the formative place of the OT is dismissed from duty in the early church. He speaks of the older scriptures as something that was added when the formal NT canonical decisions were made, viewing these scriptures as no longer intrinsically significant to the formation of the NT canon itself or the recourse made to them by the early church's deployment of the rule of faith, whose centrality he is trying to emphasize.[22]

In my judgment, appeal to the rule of faith is precisely right, but it is on terms other than Allert is seeking. A close reading of the texts reveals that the rule of faith is, as Allert indicates, that crucial piece of logical appeal (what Osborne calls an argument, and what Blowers and others see as ex-

21. Whether B. B. Warfield's understanding, as this has found its way into American evangelicalism, is continuous with the concerns of the early church is probably an important question. But using the rule of faith to obscure the centrality of the OT as a scriptural witness to the major ontological claims of the Christian faith while the NT is under development is not an advance. It fundamentally misconstrues the deeply exegetical rootage and character of the rule.

22. C. D. Allert, *A High View of Scripture? The Authority of the Bible and the Formation of the New Testament Canon*, Evangelical *Ressourcement* (Grand Rapids: Baker Academic, 2007), 41; see note 4 of the introduction, above.

egetical in character)[23] in a context when the NT is under construction. Allert does attempt to keep the perspective of von Campenhausen and others in view here, but, like von Campenhausen, we must factor in the indispensible role that the stable OT canon plays in the rule itself. The rule does understand the fragile nature, or incipient nature, of NT writings as a context for adjudication, but this is precisely because the NT's canonical authority is still in the future in a comprehensive sense—that is, in the same comprehensive sense that already accrued to the scriptures of Israel. The church fathers accept and refer with enthusiasm to this witness as grounding convictions about Jesus Christ, eternal Word, promised of old, in accordance with the Scriptures, and they do so in a way remarkably evenly distributed across its manifold books.[24] It is not the existence of this venerable authority that is at issue in the debate with opponents. The authority of the OT is not in question, nor are its contours too blurry or its formal character incomplete in some way that still requires a positive endorsement by both parties. Rather, what is at stake is how this witness confirms and substantiates the claims of the gospel. In time, debates over the actual letters of the OT witness will occur, but this is precisely because the antecedent authority of the witness is agreed upon.

23. Paul M. Blowers, "The *regula fidei* and the Narrative Character of Early Christian Faith," *ProEccl* 6 (1997): 199–228.

24. See John Behr's fine discussion in "The Tradition and Canon of the Gospel according to the Scriptures" and "The Scriptural Christ," in *The Way to Nicaea* (Crestwood, NY: St. Vladimir's Press, 2001). This issue is discussed in detail in the last two chapters of my forthcoming book, *The Character of Christian Scripture*, STI (Grand Rapids: Baker Academic). For one example among many of how crucial the scriptures of Israel are in the rule of faith, see St. Irenaeus of Lyons, *On the Apostolic Preaching*, trans. J. Behr (Crestwood, NY: St. Vladimir's Seminary Press, 1997).

So what are we to make of the existence of printed Bibles that adopt the convention of a fourfold order? Does my argument demand that the Christian church reorder its canonical OT so as to conform to the tripartite order? I am not against the fourfold order, so long as we do not draw wrong conclusions from this convention. When the fundamental logic and grammar of the tripartite structure has been grasped, it is entirely possible to understand how the fourfold order arose and indeed how a wide variety of listings emerged. Even Barton, having tried to see in a rival order a specific theological motive, acknowledges the difficulty of such a view:

> But both Sinaiticus and Alexandrinus place the prophetic books in the middle, between the histories and the poetical or didactic books—in this respect following an order which is closer to the Hebrew canon as we now know it. For Christian communities that used these codices or their descendants, the "message" that we extracted from the arrangement of the LXX was simply not available, since they knew no Bible arranged in such a way as to make it plausible.[25]

Throughout this book, I have argued that describing the non-Mosaic books as a single assortment of various prophetic witnesses misunderstands the role of early canon formation and what I have referred to as the achievement of association. I have done this in order to establish the view that the early church operated with a very thin description of its authoritative scriptural foundation. Defining "canon" in very formalistic ways and differentiating it from "Scripture" fails to appreciate how early canon formation is its own unique achievement, an achievement widely deferred to in the emerg-

25. J. Barton, *The Spirit and the Letter: Studies in the Biblical Canon* (London: SPCK, 1997), 90–91.

ing NT and assumed without much of an argument in the ante-Nicene fathers. The rule of faith is an argument based on the scriptures of Israel for maximal continuity between Christ's work and the Scriptures that promised his appearing and that spoke of his activity in figure, in word to patriarch and prophet, in moral exhortation, and in the giving of the law—all under a network of types within the OT itself.

Irenaeus provides innumerable examples of this ontological identification, as he sees it, illumining the scriptures of Israel. Speaking of Christ as Logos,

> This is He who, in the bush, spoke with Moses and said, "I have surely seen the afflictions of my people who are in Egypt, and I have come down to deliver them." This is He who ascended and descended for the salvation of the afflicted, delivering us from the dominion of the Egyptians, that is, from all idolatry and ungodliness, and saving us from the Red Sea, that is, from the deadly turbulence of the heathen and from the bitter current of their blasphemy—for in these [things] our [affairs] were pre-formed (προμελετάω), the Word of God at that time demonstrating in advance, by types, things to come, but now, truly removing us out of the cruel slavery of the heathen, He caused a stream of water to gush forth abundantly from a rock in the desert, and the rock is Himself, and [also] gave [us] twelve springs, that is, the teaching of the twelve apostles; and killing the unbelievers in the desert, while leading those who believed in Him and were infants in malice into the inheritance of the patriarchs, which, not Moses, but Jesus <gave as an inheritance>, who saves us from Amalek by stretching out His hands and leading us into the Father's Kingdom. (*Demonstration of the Apostolic Preaching* 46)[26]

26. Behr, trans., *On the Apostolic Preaching*, 70–71.

Speaking of the scriptures of Israel as but part of a wide religious literature reduces or obscures this pivotal role and creates the view that the OT comes along to join a new collection of canonical works after their character as canon has been successfully decided at a late date by the church. The instrumental role of the OT's grammar—the Law and Prophets—falls to the side, and in its place is a churchly decision to argue for certain NT writings as canon and to retain, presumably as background documents, the scriptures of Israel and other kindred works. This history-of-religion explanation is a severe reduction of what the early church confessed when it said that what Christ accomplished was "in accordance with the Scriptures."

When Brevard Childs spoke of the "search for the Christian Bible," he was referring to the discipline, the task, of Christian theological appropriation of its two-testament Bible. This discipline, or task, must be accomplished with charity and humility and with an explicit appeal to God the Holy Spirit. Childs also spoke of the Masoretic text, the tripartite canon, as the lens through which the canonical OT could best be seen or sought. This present work is an effort to explicate what I believe he meant by that. The tripartite structure is not an eternal verity or a fixed and immutable delivery system of propositions. Precisely in the accomplishment of its form, it guards against what Childs would have called "biblicism." Instead, it calls for faith, for patient listening, and for the identification of a place of obedient standing within its logic and its promise, in accordance with its form, its character, and its soaring literal sense.

Conclusion

The Goodly Fellowship of the Prophets

In a recent study of the origin of the earliest witnessing to Jesus Christ, found in mature form in the Gospels of the NT, Richard Bauckham has sought to honor a form of history writing that he calls "testimony." His emphasis is on eyewitness testimony that he judges to lie at the foundation of the literary records, as these took form in the churches of the eyewitnesses themselves.[1] He deals with an important and well-known passage from Papias in a sensitive and insightful way. He correctly asserts that the account is not setting "living testimony" above "written testimony" but rather is claiming the reliability of the former and the critical character of such testimony in anchoring the written accounts that emerge in time and that, in their own unique way, constitute the permanent testimony to Christ in the church.[2]

---

1. R. J. Bauckham, *Jesus and the Eyewitnesses* (Grand Rapids: Eerdmans, 2007).

2. *Pace* Francis Watson, *Text and Truth: Redefining Biblical Theology* (Grand Rapids: Eerdmans, 1997).

In this famous account, Papias tells of the aged Polycarp, bishop of Smyrna, relating the stories about Jesus, proud that he can recall the living testimony of those who had known the apostles. The living testimony chain—from apostles to elders to Polycarp and from Polycarp to his audience—is a significant and irreplaceable datum, grounding what Papias perceives as foundational testimony to Jesus Christ, which is soon to give way to written accounts and a growing scriptural witness taking form on analogy to the received scriptures of Israel. Given the significance of this "living testimony," one detail in the account Papias has left us becomes all the more striking. The aged Polycarp, proud of his access to apostolic witness, nevertheless relates this testimony to his audience, Papias tells us, as "in accordance with the Scriptures." That is, what can be recollected and passed on about Jesus Christ gathers its sense and encourages conviction and assent in relationship to the scriptures of Israel.[3] The mature creedal statement, going back of course to Paul's confession in 1 Cor. 15:2–4, is that the central teaching handed down (*paradosis*) about Christ's death and resurrection is "in accordance with the Scriptures." From Paul to Papias to Nicene Creed—in whatever way we might understand that evolution more precisely—the scriptural witness from Israel is a foundational and irreplaceable testimony to Jesus Christ.[4]

My argument is that to speak of these same Scriptures as distinguishable from canon runs the risk of misunderstanding this foundational conviction lying at the base of declarations

---

3. "What the things were which he had heard from them concerning the Lord, his mighty works and his teaching, Polycarp, as having received them from the eyewitnesses (*autopton*) of the life of the Logos, would declare *in accordance with the scriptures*" (Bauckham, *Jesus and the Eyewitnesses*, 35, emphasis mine).

4. C. Seitz, "'In Accordance with the Scriptures': Creed, Scripture, and 'Historical Jesus,'" in *Word without End* (Waco: Baylor University Press, 2004), 51–60.

about who Christ is and what his life, death, and resurrection are about. It moves the root conviction, found in apostolic form and grounded in a stable scriptural witness, to a later institutional decision in the church, or it regards the status of canonicity as a later development and so disallows, obscures, or attenuates what it means for the church to receive a living and authoritative witness from Israel.

Crucial to my argument is the "goodly fellowship of the prophets," that is, the achievement of association now constituted by the witness of historical prophecy (Joshua, Judges, Samuel, Kings), the book of the Twelve, and the three large-scale witnesses of Isaiah, Jeremiah, and Ezekiel. This achievement always worked in conjunction with the evolving witness of torah, or law, and took form in reciprocal relationship to it as its own maturing witness.[5] The third collection, the Writings, was its own achievement, but it did not take form on analogy to the Law or the Prophets, for its internal shape and order were differently understood. With perhaps the minor exception of the five small books constituting the Megilloth,[6] the individual books of the Writings are best understood as discrete witnesses, whose associations are external to the "division" in which they are now settled. Arguments portraying all the non-Mosaic books as diverse and wide ranging misunderstand the achievement of the Prophets and the relationship of this achievement to the Law as a single and foundational grammar. Further, they fail to understand the character of the Writings as different in kind, open to shifting order, and able to gather to themselves (in theory and consistent with their character as Writings) a

5. S. Chapman, *The Law and the Prophets: A Study in Old Testament Canon Formation*, FAT 27 (Tübingen: Mohr Siebeck, 2000).

6. A book such as Ruth may have been edited to sit next to the end of Proverbs but also to migrate in association with the movement from Judges to Samuel.

greater or lesser number of books. Improper assessment of the distinction between Law-Prophets and Writings has made the matter of closure far more important than it should be and has led to a distinction between Scripture and canon that is formalistic and inaccurate. It is semantically meaningful to speak of an "open canon," and when Paul or Polycarp or creeds use language such as "in accordance with the Scriptures," they are reckoning with the character of authority accruing to the Law and the Prophets, whether at the time in question this terminology meant a closed canon of three divisions or a twofold grammar whose additional books are in looser relationship.

In light of the recent appeal to the rule of faith as determinative in canonicity, I have also sought to emphasize that the rule in the ante-Nicene fathers required a stable and authoritative scriptural witness (which came to be called the OT) for its logic to emerge clearly. The rule is an insistence that these Scriptures ground basic Christian belief: that the creator God of the OT and the Son, or Logos, are one and that the scriptures of Israel both promise the Son's appearing, death, and resurrection and show him as active in type and shadow within the economies of God's activity in Israel. The rule is not a *discrimen* to help fix the limits of the canon but rather grows out of the logic of a single inherited Scripture whose plain sense extends to speak of Christ as it speaks of historical action, promise, moral exhortation, law, and final purpose with Israel and the nations within the literary compass of the Law and the Prophets.

If the scriptural, or canonical, authority of the OT as Christian Scripture is properly grasped, the use of the Scriptures within the literary development and mature form of the

NT will likewise be rightly understood. In reconstructions of the canon that emphasize the centrality of the NT and only secondarily the OT, there is the danger that the contribution of the scriptures of Israel as a canonical reality will be lost. The NT makes clear that with statements of confession, it is impossible to understand the person and work of Christ apart from the logic of accordance with the OT. The canonicity of the NT is an analogous and derivative phenomenon, taking its logic and bearings from the existence of an anterior witness in a given material form. At the level of biblical theology, the OT speaks of Christ in accordance with its own plain sense presentation, in the light of economic confessions as to its *telos*. This is not the same thing as imitating the use of the Old in the New but rather entails basic convictions as to the theological claims of the OT to speak of God. The rule of faith is the assertion that the work of God in the scriptures of Israel promises, foreshadows, typifies, and grounds what it means to speak of Christ as Son of God and the one who will come again as judge, the two advents promised by the selfsame witness.

As a result of the present work, my hope is that the grounding character of the scriptures of Israel will be better appreciated, especially at a time when historical developmentalism forms the overdetermined backdrop against which we read both the Old and the New Testaments of one Christian Scripture. Even within the maturation of the first scriptural witness, Law and Prophets are not successive phases in a history of religion but belong together as a reciprocal account of God's providential work in creation, law, and historical action in Israel and the nations, including future promise, the fulfillment of God's righteous will, and new creation. This same dynamic governs the way the Old and the New now work together, a single canonical totality dynamically related and mutually informing. The New is not a phase of development that grounds the Old but rather a statement of the Old's abiding sense and final meaning, perceived now afresh within its own plain-sense deliverances and helping to interpret and ground the New's meaning and final purpose as well.

Index